YOUR
SMALL
BUSINESS
BLUEPRINT

AN ENTREPRENEUR'S STEP-BY-STEP
GUIDE TO BUILDING A SUCCESSFUL
STARTUP FROM THE GROUND UP

HACK
Learning
LIFE

RON NEARY

Your Small Business Blueprint
© 2025 by Times 10 Publications
Highland Heights, OH 44143 USA
Website: 10publications.com

All web links in this book are correct as of the publication date but may have become inactive or otherwise modified since that time. Name brands should not be considered endorsements by the author or Times 10 Publications.

Cover and Interior Design by Steven Plummer
Project Management by Regina Bell
Editing by Tarah Threadgill
Copyediting by Jennifer Jas

Paperback ISBN: 978-1-956512-65-6
eBook ISBN: 978-1-956512-67-0
Hardcover ISBN: 978-1-956512-66-3

Library of Congress Cataloging-in-Publication Data is available for this title.

First Printing: March 2025

Mom and Dad

Thank you for showing me the dignity of hard work.

Connie Hamilton

Thank you for challenging me to write this book and to be the best version of myself.

Our Men and Women in Uniform

You are my heroes.

TABLE OF CONTENTS

INTRODUCTION

FROM BLUEPRINT TO MOVE-IN

The road to success is always under construction.
— ARNOLD PALMER, PROFESSIONAL GOLFER

YOU DO NOT need a business degree to successfully plan, structure, launch, and move a new business into its early growth stage. Many of us who dream of starting a business are motivated by a great idea and the opportunity to work for ourselves, manage our schedules, make our own decisions, make more money, and make a difference.

Whatever your motivation, *Your Small Business Blueprint* offers a straightforward, step-by-step framework to build your startup, help you discover what works best for you, and ensure your dream becomes a reality.

A simple analogy to building a startup business is the process of constructing a new home. From the design layout in the blueprints to the construction, the final inspection, and the move-in day, there is a sequence of steps every contractor must follow to build a new home successfully.

From an early age, I started working in construction with my dad. My brothers and I were often "voluntold" to participate as general laborers. We were on many crews: roofing shingle tear-off crew, garage paint crew, trench digging crew, landscape crew, fall cleanup crew, snow removal crew, you name the crew where simple, low-risk labor was needed, and chances are high that we were on it. The three of us were cheap labor and, I like to think, a productive crew (most of the time) for our foreman (Dad).

"DRIVING TRUCK"

Just as building a business from the ground up can throw unexpected challenges your way, there was a moment during my childhood construction experience when I quickly realized I was entirely unprepared. One fall Saturday, Dad asked us if we were interested in being part of the crew for the sidewalk project at the family lake cottage. He explained that new sidewalks were being poured and we would get to "drive truck" during the day of the project. The sidewalks were long and led out to the lake. I remember telling my brother Joe, "Hey, we get to drive trucks!"

We were in our mid-teens, and I assumed we would get to drive some type of mechanized vehicles hauling concrete for the new sidewalks. I convinced Joe that getting to "drive truck" would be fun and we shouldn't miss the opportunity to spend the day at the lake doing something cool. Joe was skeptical but eventually agreed, and we told Dad we were in for "driving truck." When we arrived at the lake cottage, the forms were already in place for the concrete pour and other family members and friends were busy working and prepping for the arrival of the cement truck. I noticed a line of wheelbarrows near the street, and being excited to "drive truck," I looked around for the mysterious mechanized trucks we would be driving. Dad gathered a few of us for a short briefing on what to do when the cement truck arrived. He explained that we would need to work quickly and accurately and keep the supply of concrete moving to complete the pour of the new sidewalk. He also told us not to spill any concrete in the grass, or we would have "one hell of a mess to clean up." At that moment, I realized that "driving truck" meant pushing a wheelbarrow full of concrete.

By the end of the day, my brother and I were exhausted and our arms were so sore that I thought they might fall off. The good news is that we did not spill any concrete and did not slow down the process too much. The bad news is that I was *way off* in my understanding of what it meant to "drive truck."

I had every opportunity to ask Dad for clarification and learn more details about the project and tasks, but as a fourteen-year-old, it sounded so cool that I made assumptions, had my own ideas about what it meant, and eagerly volunteered to participate as part of the concrete sidewalk crew of 1984. Dad was tough but fair, and that day remains a learning milestone in my early work life. I learned to question and confirm the detailed game plan and deliverables for any projects that came my way.

To pay for college, I worked in construction as a general laborer, stepping into roles as a carpenter, painter, landscaper, plumber, roofer, and more to keep projects on schedule. The owner, a supportive boss, was flexible with my class schedule and ensured I had as many work hours as needed. When work was slow, he connected me with other builders, allowing me to learn diverse construction methods and improve my efficiency. This experience conditioned me to seek better ways of doing things—a mindset I've carried into my professional life after college.

As my career progressed, I found myself in many different business roles, from working in large, publicly traded Fortune 500 organizations with thousands of employees, to mid-size companies looking for the next phase of exponential growth, to smaller companies with lofty goals of reaching the next growth milestone in their company life cycle. I evolved into a "fix-it-man" and a "change agent," conditioned to relentlessly seek the root cause of business challenges and search for elusive insights on solutions to get the business back on track and improve financial performance.

Interestingly, the term "voluntold" made a comeback. I often heard, "Give it to Neary; he'll figure it out" or "Let Neary handle it; he might drive everyone crazy, but he'll get it done." In response to the question, "Is he qualified to lead this business?" my response was, "I'm not sure and don't have much experience in this field, but we'll learn and figure it out together."

What is different and unique about the *Your Small Business Blueprint* approach is that my career experience and drive to "figure it out" have led me to be mindful of three lessons when "voluntold":

1. Learning never stops.

2. Change is constant.

3. Continuous improvement is, well, continuous.

These three lessons will resonate repeatedly as you work through *Your Small Business Blueprint*. Starting a new business is about learning and adapting to change and continuously improving as you engage with customers and move into the early growth stage of your business. Change is constant, and it is up to *you* to be mindful of these three lessons to qualify what you have learned and adapt yourself and your business to be successful and profitable.

My inspiration to write and curate a book about the steps of structuring and launching a startup business came from the unique perspectives of all the crew leaders, business leaders, veterans, military service members, and teammates I learned from, especially those who had the confidence to look at me and say, "You'll figure it out." They gave me the latitude to learn from my mistakes, challenge the status quo, push limits, and try new things, and they had the patience to answer when I constantly asked, "Why?"

THE HACK LEARNING FORMULA

The Hack Learning Life Series formula is the perfect format to guide you through the sequential process of structuring and launching your new business into its early growth stage. It fosters a pragmatic, step-by-step approach with practical solutions that you can workshop to address the key elements of your vision and ideas to develop a winning plan of action for your new business:

- The Problem – A specific startup business challenge.

- The Hack – A clearly stated solution to the challenge.

- What You Can Do Tomorrow – Action items you can use right away to get started.

- Building Momentum – Workshop strategies to establish foundational structures.

- Removing Obstacles – Answers to common questions and roadblocks.

- The Hack in Action – A real-world example of small businesses deploying the strategy.

How to Use This Book: From Blueprint to Move-In

Your Small Business Blueprint is a sequential roadmap for successfully constructing your startup's critical elements. I recommend that you read each Hack (chapter) in its entirety to understand how to implement each step. Then, grab a pen and paper (or digital device), and workshop your startup idea through each Hack in chronological order.

Look at each Hack as a milestone. By objective confirmation, decide if you have successfully completed the current Hack and are confident and fully prepared to move on to the next one.

Look for the checklists at the end of each Hack and answer each question to confirm you are ready to move to the next step in the process. Additionally, visit my website, ronneary.com, to access free resources and tools to help you organize and work through the blueprint steps to successfully construct your startup.

HACK 1

DRAFT YOUR BLUEPRINT
Do Your Homework and Get Organized

Plans are only good intentions unless they immediately degenerate into hard work.
— PETER DRUCKER, MANAGEMENT CONSULTANT, EDUCATOR, AND AUTHOR

THE PROBLEM: YOU'RE NOT SURE WHERE TO BEGIN

MAGINE IF A builder started building your new dream home without a blueprint and plan, expecting to complete a successful build on schedule and within budget. After witnessing problems in delays, cost overruns, and missed steps, you would probably question their approach and wonder if they were competent enough to finish the job.

Not being sure where to begin when constructing a startup business can also lead to problems, such as not clearly defining your product or service and not identifying your ideal customer and their needs and expectations. A lack of understanding of the industry, market, and direct competitors can also lead to missteps that will diminish your opportunity to launch a successful business.

Like building a home, starting a business can feel overwhelming with all the decisions and steps in the construction process to connect and perform in the right order. A new entrepreneur is like a home builder in that they can imagine the finished product but may fail to do their homework and follow the blueprint to ensure a successful build.

THE HACK: DRAFT YOUR BLUEPRINT

An excellent way to get organized is to start with a simple description of your product or service. This is your first step in capturing important details and addressing the basics in a checklist of factors to consider and research.

Remember that this will be a living document that will evolve as you research, learn, and develop the blueprint of how your new business will deliver your solution to customers and how it can be positioned as different and better than the competition. The definition of your product or service is a baseline to build on while constructing the other elements of your new business. Consider the following product definition checklist, including descriptions of each category, to help you think about your business blueprint. Remember, each category is subject to change, so document your ideas now and know you can change them later. For a downloadable version of this checklist, visit ronneary.com.

Product Definition Checklist

1. *Product/Service Definition:* An overview of your product or service. Describe the "What" in a simple sentence or short paragraph. What is it?

2. *Customer Profile:* The end user who will benefit from your product or service. Who is your ideal customer?

3. *Features and Benefits:* A feature is an essential function or component of your product or service. A benefit describes your product or service and how it can make the consumer's life easier or better.

4. *Customer Requirements:* The critical elements or necessities of a product or service that will motivate a customer to buy. Put yourself in the customer's place: What are the minimum features you want when buying a product or service?

5. *Warranty/Guarantee Expectations:* The durability and reliability of your product or service, including expectations of the quality or how long it should reasonably last. Consider a common-sense understanding of what is fair and reasonable.

6. *Competitive Advantages and Disadvantages:* What makes your product or service different and better? These initial thoughts will be adjusted and refined as you move through *Your Small Business Blueprint.*

7. *Targeted Channels of Distribution:* How will you get your product or service to the consumer as quickly and efficiently as possible? You have many factors to consider, such as:

- ► Are you selling directly to consumers or other businesses?
- ► How do competitive businesses sell their products or services? Is there a standard method of delivery in the industry?
- ► Will the customer purchase online? Will they need to touch and feel the product before purchasing?
- ► What is the customer's requirement for the speed of delivery?

8. *Sales Forecast:* A projection of how many units of your product or service you believe you can sell in a given time. It is valuable to think broadly in terms of a year, but for simplicity, start by looking at one month and ask the following questions:

- ► How many units can you sell in a month?
- ► How many units can you deliver in a month?

9. *Number of Offerings:* The number of different products or services you will make available to customers to buy in your business.

10. *Timing Requirements:* A sequential list of milestone tasks you must accomplish leading up to your product or service launch.

11. *Still to Do:* A simple list of open items you need to address as you work through the process of creating your product or service. Think of this in the context of a brain-storming exercise.

WHAT YOU CAN DO TOMORROW

Focus on the basics. Explore and learn about the current state of the industry and comparable solutions. Even if you have experience and expertise in your industry, market, or local area where you will conduct business, remember that changes and innovations are constant. What you find may inspire your vision of developing a different and better solution.

- **Set aside time for homework.** Write it down, set reminders, and don't expect to do it all in one day. Spend dedicated time working on each element in the product definition checklist as it relates to your proposed product or service idea. As a new entrepreneur, your passion to be successful has your mind racing as you think about all the different aspects of the business. As for me, I never know when an idea or thought will resonate, so I carry a notebook to write down my thoughts so I can revisit them and develop the idea further in my dedicated time.

- **Start looking like a customer.** To identify comparable solutions, search for a similar product or service as if you are a customer. Research the market with a simple online search for your product or service, including keywords and phrases. In Hack 2, you will do a deeper dive. For now, explore and see what's out there. For example, if I wanted to start a food truck business in my hometown, my search might look like this:

Local market and comparable solution research key phrases

- ▸ Best food truck near me
- ▸ Best BBQ food truck near me (specific to your primary food interest)
- ▸ Highest-rated food truck near me
- ▸ 3 keys to a successful food truck business in (your target city)
- ▸ What permits are needed for a food truck in (your city and state)

- **Take a first look at the industry.** Think of this as a broad look to understand the industry for your product or service. Is the industry growing? Is there a demand for your product or service? What is new and trending? Are emerging technologies, processes, and delivery methods improving efficiency and

the customer experience? What are the distribution channels, and how do customers buy
and receive delivery of the product or service? A simple online search is a good place
to start.

NAIL IT:

Research broad key phrases
to find information on the
industry and market you
want to learn more about.

Key phrase examples to research

- ▶ Top ten growth trends
- ▶ Related trade associations and publications
- ▶ Industry technology and equipment trends
- ▶ Best related business in other states
- ▶ Most effective methods to promote my business

- **Find examples for inspiration.** This is your opportunity to identify other businesses that offer a similar solution and begin to gain knowledge of the features and benefits of their products and services. These are not companies you will compete with directly, but they operate in other markets and offer valuable examples you may want to emulate for your startup. You may even reach out to them and develop a relationship for advice and future collaboration.

BUILDING MOMENTUM

Building momentum in this first step is not about finalizing the elements of your proposed product or service. Instead, it's about organizing and capturing your thoughts, beliefs, and convictions and conducting basic research on the industry, market, and competitors. This groundwork will enable a more detailed market analysis in Hack 2.

STEP 1: Identify direct competitor market leaders.

It is valuable to find direct competitor benchmarks for comparison. Typically, you can find two or three strong competitors (referred to as market leaders) to use as an initial basis for comparing your solution's defined "must-haves." If you conduct business in a specific geographic area, such as your local city, it will be easy to identify key direct competitors.

STEP 2: Fill out the product definition checklist.

Outline and capture your thoughts for each of the eleven elements in the product definition checklist as they relate to your solution. Think of defining these elements as a first draft to capture and organize your thoughts. This will give you a starting point to compare, contrast, and adjust your research to develop your strategy of how your solution is different and better.

STEP 3: Dig deeper into your search results.

The information available today relative to your product or service is both plentiful and valuable. However, it's a good practice to review several results from your search and not just the first to appear in your search results. The results that appear first are typically companies that have paid to appear higher in the results and may not offer you the best information. It is good to identify multiple sources for a broader comparison.

STEP 4: Refine your checklist.

As an organized starting point and living document, a well-thought-out description of your ideal product or service will include a sales forecast, number of offerings, timing, and list of tasks yet to be done. You'll need to refine the details as you develop your idea.

REMOVING OBSTACLES

In today's business world, innovation is constant and change happens at lightning speed. Whether you have years of experience or are new to the industry and market, there is a risk of getting into a situation I have often experienced: **analysis paralysis.** Here are a few common questions and my responses.

Am I overthinking? Analysis paralysis refers to excessive analysis leading to overthinking, inaction, or the inability to decide and take action. Information is so easily and readily accessible that when someone is so focused on gathering data, analyzing every detail, or considering every possible outcome, they might become overwhelmed and unable to move forward. It can hinder progress, productivity, and decision-making. Balancing analysis with action is critical in this first step of outlining your solution, leading to successive milestones as we work through the steps of *Your Small Business Blueprint.*

What if I don't know the answer to one of the items on the checklist? It is frustrating when you can't find a confident answer to a question. We tend to want to confirm the correct answer no matter how long it takes. Remember that this will be a living document, and you will inevitably revise it as you work through the process of creating your best solution. I recommend that you fill in your best answer and include an asterisk or question mark to identify that you will need to revisit it for improvement.

What if I don't have enough money to get started? Having enough money is a stressful concern for sure. Permit yourself to set aside this concern as you decide on the layout and design for your startup. In this early stage, your primary investment is the time and energy it takes to do your homework and get organized. Later, we will address how to fund your business in Hack 10.

What if I struggle to validate the findings in my market research? It is okay to be wrong. Learning never stops, and change is constant. Rather than consider it wrong, think of it as a starting point for continuous improvement. What you can do is enlist feedback. Reach out to a trusted colleague or friend and share your product definition checklist. Ask for their perspective, additional considerations, and areas of concern. Remember, those who don't make mistakes miss the opportunity to learn.

THE HACK IN ACTION

My friend Chris spends his summers at a beautiful lake in Northern Michigan that attracts boaters and vacationers in the summer months. The lake is quite large, being almost twenty-two miles long. It includes lakefront cottages and a few spots to dock your boat and venture inland to enjoy a nice meal and recharge before heading back out on the lake for more summer fun. The lake has a large sandbar at the south end that has become a gathering spot for boaters to anchor, relax, swim, and enjoy the warm sun and cool blue water.

Chris wondered if there was an opportunity to offer food and beverages to boaters without them having to leave the sandbar and interrupt their day of fun on the water. He came up with the idea to convert a pontoon raft into an aquatic food truck that could anchor on the sandbar and serve a menu of delicious food items, drinks, and treats to the hungry boaters.

Chris researched the possibilities and used the product definition checklist to outline and organize his idea into a plan. He found that mobile food trucks are trending and popular as small-business startups. The following is a product definition checklist for the aquatic food truck that Chris put together.

Chris's Product Definition Checklist

Service Definition: Aquatic food truck offering food and drinks.
Customer Profile: Ideal customers are boaters anchored at the sandbar.

Features & Benefits:

Features: Service window; gas grills; refrigerator; freezer; storage for snacks, drinks, buns, condiments, and paper products; refuse container; battery or generator power for refrigerator/freezer.
Benefits: Location, location, location. Conveniently bringing food and drinks to the sandbar. Boaters do not have to leave or lose their anchor spot on the sandbar. Allows customers to satisfy their hunger and thirst and continue enjoying the summer day.

Customer Requirements: All about the menu:
Sandwiches – grilled chicken, burgers, hot dogs
Snacks – various snack chip options
Sweet treats – cookies, candy, ice cream bars, popsicles
Drinks – Bottled water, various canned sodas

Warranty/Guarantee Expectations: Fresh and hot sandwiches. Cold drinks.

Competitive Advantages & Disadvantages:

Advantages – Conveniently located on the sandbar. Customers do not have to interrupt their day to get food and drink.
Disadvantages – Limited menu options. Inclement weather will negatively impact business.

Targeted Channels of Distribution:

- Direct sales to consumers.
- Develop a name for the business with a simple website.
- Allow customers to pay with cash or with credit cards.
- What other products could we offer? (sunscreen, cool water toys, kayak or jet ski rentals)
- Wait time for customers will need to be short for hot sandwiches.

Sales Forecast:

- Summer season – Memorial Day to Labor Day, three months.
- Weekly schedule – Plan one fully stocked trip on Monday, Tuesday, and Wednesday based on traffic on the sandbar. Plan two fully stocked trips on Thursday, Friday, Saturday, and Sunday.
- Daily hours – 11 a.m. to 5 p.m., weather permitting.
- Difficult to forecast based on individual menu items.
- Base the sales forecast on the capacity of items that can be stocked on the pontoon and the number of trips to the sandbar per day after returning to the dock to restock. There may be hotter weekend days in July and August when three fully stocked trips may be required.

Number of Offerings: Some items may vary based on supplier availability and pricing (snacks, drinks, ice cream, popsicles).

Timing Requirements:

December – Complete purchase of pontoon raft platform.
January – Complete design of aquatic food truck build.
February – Complete purchase of service equipment.
March – Complete build of aquatic food truck.
April – Gain US Coast Guard approval. Launch website.
May – Finalize menu and supplies.
Launch date – Saturday of Memorial Day weekend.

Still to Do:

- Determine whether it makes sense to offer other items and rentals.
- Staffing plan and licensing requirements to operate food truck.
- Finalize business name, colors, branding, and logo.
- Determine business banking, loan/credit, and legal structure.
- Costs and pricing for sale items, and profit potential.

Chris was a schoolteacher, and this would be his summer side job. He was pleased to have a checklist to define and organize his business idea, identify open items to address, and establish timing requirements to fully capitalize on a seasonal summer business. He felt confident he had a successful start to his first year operating an aquatic food truck.

I firmly believe in "fast-track development," meaning setting a reasonable timeline to develop your solution, execute your plan, and get your product or service into the marketplace. Consider the Apple iPhone. Apple did not envision the iPhone 15 and then pass on launching the first fourteen versions of the phone. They launched the first iPhone and, learning from user feedback, made incremental improvements to the product and its features, leading to the best version we have today. The key takeaway is that once you have defined your product or solution, commit to the launch date to get your product or service to customers so you can begin to measure, learn, gain insight, and identify improvements to make in the next version. Innovation is constant in today's business world, and change happens at lightning speed.

The new entrepreneur sees a need or problem and has a unique or better solution. In Hack 2, "Lay a Solid Foundation," we will do a much deeper dive into strategies to research the market and competitors.

The process of doing your homework and getting organized is simple. Do what you can to be prepared and make good choices. The next page shows a checklist (you'll find one at the end of each Hack) to help you stay organized with your progress. Visit the Resources page on ronneary. com to find more downloadable lists.

HACK 1
DRAFT YOUR BLUEPRINT

Completed

Have you completed the Product
Definition Checklist for your solution?

Do you have a current understanding of
the industry and your market?

Have you identified two or three direct
competitor market leaders?

Are you prepared to move to the next
phase of construction?

LAY A SOLID FOUNDATION
Scope Out the Market

There is no competition in the world. If you can start something, carry it through, and complete it, you are in the 2 percent of our society.

— JOHN SAVAGE, BUSINESSMAN AND AUTHOR

THE PROBLEM: YOU DON'T KNOW WHAT YOU DON'T KNOW

I N THE CONSTRUCTION world, the home's foundation supports everything built on top of it. So, imagine if your builder did not prep the site by testing the soil, clearing rocks and debris, leveling the ground, addressing the drainage plan to prevent water damage, calculating load bearing to ensure the foundation can support the weight of the structure, and determining the right materials for the strength of the foundation. Your new home would experience cracked walls, stuck windows and doors that won't operate properly, leaks in the plumbing, uneven floors, and quite possibly a cracked or failing foundation. As a home buyer, you would question why the prep work was not done thoroughly so that the foundation could support the entire house being built on top of it.

Not having a clear and detailed understanding of the market in which you intend to build your business can also lead to significant problems. Potential "cracks in the foundation" that could hinder your future success include not differentiating your business from tough competitors, lacking an understanding of your value to customers, incorrectly pricing your products or services, missing out on trends or new technologies that you could use to your advantage, and not recognizing the strengths and threats of a competitor that could compromise your business.

Not gaining a foundational understanding of your market can lead to unknowingly making the wrong decisions, which can result in the inevitable downfall of your business before you can even get it up and running.

THE HACK: LAY A SOLID FOUNDATION

Delve deeper into determining your direct competitors, learning who offers the best product or service today, and understanding their go-to-market strategies. This is necessary because you need to create and position your business to stand out and appeal to customers so they will choose you over your competitors.

Now that you have done the essential industry and market research, identified a couple of strong competitors, and developed a definition of your product or service, you can conduct a more detailed analysis of the market and your competitors.

Your market position refers to how you will differentiate your business from customers in the market relative to your competitors. It includes how you price your product or service, how customers perceive your brand, who your ideal target customers are, and the value proposition (what is most important) to the customer for the unique benefits of your solution. Thinking through these areas is vital because when you understand your direct competitors' strengths and weaknesses, the insights will help you find your best market position.

Many tools are available to help you conduct a deeper dive into the competitors and target customers in the market in which your business will operate. In today's digital age, you can put advanced tools to work that complement more traditional market research tools.

Using a combination of advanced and traditional tools is an effective and thorough method for scoping out the market. This method provokes strategic thinking as you compare and prepare your best solutions to launch your new business.

Using both advanced and traditional market research tools provides a check-and-balance against putting too much weight into one source. Many people do a simple online search and accept their findings as accurate facts; however, a deep dive incorporating multiple advanced and traditional tools will validate your findings. Here is a list of potential traditional and advanced tools, including what information will help you the most.

Traditional Tools	Advanced Tools
Competitor websites and social media	Google Alerts
SWOT analyses	Revenue searches
Industry market reports	Website traffic analytics
Industry trade publications	Social media monitoring
Trade shows and conferences	Review platforms
Industry associations	Price monitoring tools

TRADITIONAL TOOLS

Competitor websites and social media are excellent ways to learn about an individual competitor. Information is so easy to access about products, services, blogs, company values, mission statements, and their stated value proposition for their products and services. Social media (such as Facebook, Instagram, LinkedIn, X, TikTok, and blog sites) can provide a sense of the people, culture, and employee experiences and perspectives. Some companies also have a YouTube channel providing tutorials, product instruction details, best practices, and other interactive information. As easily accessible as the information is on a competitor's website, remember that these are the "basics" and you can gain many more details about the company when you use advanced analysis tools.

SWOT analyses (Strengths, Weaknesses, Opportunities, and Threats) are a simple, effective method for evaluating competitors compared to your business. (See Table 2.1.) You complete the evaluation by using advanced tools to research potential competitors and answering the questions in the criteria examples that follow. Strengths and Weaknesses are internal company attributes, while Opportunities and Threats are external factors that can positively or negatively impact the business's future performance. It is helpful to think of a SWOT analysis in terms of thought-provoking criteria examples to identify the strengths, weaknesses, opportunities, and threats that can affect the business. The value of a SWOT analysis is the comparison of competitor companies to your business. A SWOT analysis template is available at ronneary.com under Resources.

SWOT Analysis Template

Strengths	Weaknesses
Opportunities	Threats

Table 2.1

SWOT ANALYSIS WITH CRITERIA EXAMPLES

STRENGTHS

Advantages of proposition
Capabilities
Competitive advantages
USPs (unique selling points)
Resources, assets, people
Experience, knowledge, data
Financial reserves, likely returns
Marketing – reach, distribution, awareness
Innovative aspects
Location and geographical
Price, value, quality
Accreditations, qualifications, certifications
Processes, systems, IT, communications
Cultural, attitudinal, behavioral
Management cover, succession
Philosophy and values

WEAKNESSES

Disadvantages of proposition
Gaps in capabilities
Lack of competitive strength
Reputation, presence, reach
Financials
Own known vulnerabilities
Timescales, deadlines, and pressures
Cash flow, startup cash-drain
Continuity, supply chain robustness
Effects on core activities, distractions
Reliability of data, plan productivity
Morale, commitment, leadership
Accreditations
Processes and systems, etc.
Management cover, succession

OPPORTUNITIES

Market developments
Competitors' vulnerabilities
Industry or lifestyle trends
Technology development and innovation
Global influences
New markets: vertical, horizontal
Niche target markets
Geographical, export, import
New USPs
Tactics, e.g., surprise, major contracts
Business and product development
Information and research
Partnerships, agencies, distribution
Volumes, production, economies
Seasonal, weather, fashion influences

THREATS

Political effects
Legislative effects
Environmental effects
IT developments
Competitor intentions
Market demand
New technologies, services, ideas
Vital contracts and partners
Sustaining internal capabilities
Obstacles faced
Insurmountable weaknesses
Loss of key staff
Sustainable financial backing
Economy – home, abroad
Seasonality, weather effects

Table 2.2

Industry market reports are valuable tools and easy to find with an online search for industry market reports for your product or service, especially in larger established industries. They are typically produced annually and updated monthly or quarterly. They provide insight into the current state of the industry, macroeconomic impacts, market leaders, industry trends, multiyear growth outlook, and geographic area-specific market information. It can be expensive to purchase an entire market report, but typically, you can get a summary and sample information at no cost. It is valuable to compare a couple of different market reports because they may include subjective interpretations in the summaries, especially regarding forecasting growth trends.

Industry trade publications are available through email subscriptions. Many are published online, and you can also get them in print if you prefer. They are typically offered at no cost and provide regular updates on the state of the industry. Features include product or service spotlights and articles by industry experts on marketing, sales trends, emerging technology tools, and features on innovative and successful companies. They offer you value by helping you monitor the industry performance so you can adjust your business for greater improvement.

Trade shows and conferences can be valuable for networking with other companies and finding vendors (suppliers) to support your business's product or service delivery. The cost of registering and attending conferences and trade shows, plus the dedicated investment of your time away from your regular business activities, is an investment in your business. It allows you to visit and see potential competitors putting their best on display for the coming business year and promoting future products. Do your homework before attending so you can identify the attendee companies on display that you are most interested in learning more about or the speakers for sessions and workshops you would like to attend.

Industry associations are often national with regional, state, and local chapters. In these organizations, you can learn, network, and participate in ideas and activities related to your industry, specifically in your local market. Many associations conduct regular meetings and ask for participation in committees and events. Think about how you might participate in a local association and ask yourself these key questions:

- How much do I want to share about myself and my business with competitors and other market participants?

- How active and at what level of participation am I willing to commit to in my local chapter?

- Is there a tangible business value for my business through my participation?

- Last, my time is valuable, so what is the opportunity cost of my time involved in participating?

The value you get from an industry association depends on what you put into it, so consider it carefully.

ADVANCED TOOLS

Google Alerts are an effective way to stay current on competitors, products, industry news, and market updates. You can set up alerts for your competitors' names and keywords related to your business and receive real-time updates. Think of a Google Alert as an automated Google search that regularly and conveniently sends you updates. Simply type in "Create an alert on Google," and you will find the steps to set it up.

Revenue searches are a valuable tool to learn about competitors. Most companies are private and do not publicly share their sales revenue or other key information. However, you can still find valuable details in public records. ZoomInfo is a simple and effective tool that offers comprehensive company information on annual revenue, key leaders and decision-makers, the year they were founded, defined industries where they conduct their business, and competitors. I have found revenue verification to be one of the most valuable tools to help identify a competitor's size and potential strength. This knowledge helps inform my go-to-market strategy and even my customer value proposition compared to competitors.

Website traffic analytics are tools that monitor the effectiveness of competitor websites, digital marketing initiatives, and keyword search engine optimization to help customers find their companies more easily when searching for products or services. They are also helpful tools for your business to compare and contrast the effectiveness of your website, online presence, and marketing efforts. Website traffic tools like Semrush, Ahrefs, and Serpstat are easy to use and can help you maximize your online presence while keeping pace with or staying ahead of your competitors.

Social media monitoring, like website traffic tools, is also an effective tool to help track competitors' social media activities, engagement metrics, and audience sentiment. Tools such as Hootsuite, Brandwatch, and Sprout Social are helpful for competitive analyses to see what is working for potential competitors' social media presence and campaigns and to provide insights as you decide which social media platforms are best to represent your business, initiate campaigns, and build followers.

Review platforms provide intel about a competitor from the customer's perspective. Formal review platforms such as Yelp, Google Reviews, or industry-specific review sites provide detailed customer perceptions of competitors' products or services. Social media monitoring can also be a resource for customer reviews. Most customers share their experiences (especially poor experiences) or openly share comments about a similar experience shared by other customers. Social media reviews are more informal and faster for customers to share their thoughts. Reviewing comments on social media can provide information about a competitor that does not offer prepared surveys, and it's a fantastic way to understand what customers appreciate or find lacking in their experiences with your potential competitors.

Price monitoring tools help track competitors' pricing strategies and changes. The real value of these tools lies in their ability to provide timely and accurate data to make informed decisions, stay competitive, and optimize your pricing strategies to maximize sales revenue and profit margins. Tools such as Prisync and Price2Spy offer dynamic pricing that allows you to adjust prices in real time based on factors such as competitor pricing, demand, and even seasonality. It's a myth that the price is the number-one driver in buying decisions for most products and services. In Hack 8, we will take a closer look at the customer's mindset in deciding to buy based on price versus value.

WHAT YOU CAN DO TOMORROW

We have reviewed twelve market research tools. To get started with putting them to work for you, try a combination of traditional and advanced tools.

- **Build competitor files.** Create and dedicate an electronic file for each competitor to organize the data. You can also create a physical file and add printed marketing materials or even a sample of their product, if possible.

- **Start with the traditional basics.** Monitoring competitors' websites and social media is a must. The SWOT analysis template in Table 2.1 is a good way to organize details. Use the criteria examples in Table 2.2 as a guide as you research your competitors' businesses.

- **Try two advanced tools.** Now that you've identified key competitors, deploy two advanced tools for competitor introspection. If you struggle to choose two advanced tools, I highly recommend ZoomInfo revenue search and Semrush web traffic analytics. Many advanced tools are available via paid subscriptions, but you can get no-cost trials for your initial competitor evaluation and then decide if a subscription fits in your budget.

BUILDING MOMENTUM

As you scope out the market, approach this process as a type of "discovery learning" with an objective and open mind. The goal is to develop a unique go-to-market strategy for your business and your customer value proposition.

STEP 1: Stay up to date with industry trends.

Industry publications are invaluable sources for staying current in the industry. Regular market condition updates and expert insights on the industry can trigger ideas and areas for focus in your business.

Nail It:

Remember to remain objective when researching industry trends or looking at competitors' strategies.

STEP 2: Conduct balanced comparisons.

Now that you have identified key direct competitors, consistently apply the traditional and advanced market research tools to each competitor. An equitable comparison will give you a balanced evaluation of all competitors.

STEP 3: Write a rough draft of your customer value proposition.

Based on the comprehensive information you are learning about customer requirements, their needs and wants, and what your competitors do well and not so well, you can begin to list the unique and valuable benefits you need to provide to make your product or service different and better than your competitors.

Your customer value proposition (CVP) describes the unique benefits that your company promises to deliver to its customers. Developing a compelling CVP involves learning about and understanding your customers' needs. It defines your unique selling points, explains why customers should buy a product or service from your company instead of other companies, and clearly articulates the value you provide.

REMOVING OBSTACLES

With all the available research and tools to learn about competitors as you differentiate your business, products, and services, it may feel like scoping out the market creates the "paralysis by analysis" we referred to in Hack 1. Your competition is changing constantly, and they will also be looking at your business when you emerge as a viable competitor in their markets. Here are common questions I hear about this stage, followed by my answers.

How do I know when I am done scoping out the market? You are never done. Scoping out the market is an ongoing exercise to stay current on your industry and markets. However, the time involved may lessen as you stay on top of it. Scoping out the market becomes second nature as your knowledge grows and you become ingrained as a member of the industry and markets in which you compete. Be patient with this process; over time, your eye for competitors' strategies and market trends grows keener, making your analysis and reactions more immediate.

Do the traditional and advanced tools apply to all industries and potential businesses? Starting up a business is not a one-size-fits-all endeavor, although the foundational steps are the same. Each business model has special considerations depending on the type of product or service you're interested in. Local businesses such as neighborhood family-owned restaurants, corner stores, or bakeries focus on specific customers in small, local markets. Also, unique customized products may have a niche market, such as handmade jewelry or other craft-type businesses that may benefit more from research based on customer interactions and local events than traditional and advanced market research tools. This does not mean those business owners can slack on doing their due diligence in learning about direct competitors, considering economic conditions, and taking advantage of opportunities (the volume of ideal target customers) by scoping out the market.

With so much research and information, how do I avoid analysis paralysis? Two critical actions can help you avoid falling into this trap: get organized and commit to a regular schedule of researching the current industry, market updates, and key direct competitors. Once you have established a baseline for your comprehensive findings, it is time to act—to develop and launch your new business—based on what you have learned.

What if I am unsure of my market position and how my business is different? The primary goal of scoping out the market is to learn how to differentiate your business and appeal to your ideal customers. You can only determine this once you know who offers similar products or services. You will better understand your market position and develop your unique identity (your brand) as you proceed through the Hacks. You'll want to pay particular attention to Hack 8 regarding your marketing plan.

Nail It:

When you launch your new business, you will be focused on day-to-day activities to keep it running successfully. The natural tendency is to become internally focused. A good practice is to simply put a recurring task or reminder on your calendar to dedicate an hour twice a month to scoping out the market by checking in on industry trends, the current state of the market, and what is new with key direct competitors.

THE HACK IN ACTION

Mike and Tim, working together, developed a new type of barnwood wall covering that is different from other products, and they both believed from their industry experience that there could be many advantages to their product. They also learned that reclaimed barnwood is a hot trend in interior design and a fast-growing market, offering a timely opportunity for their new product.

While scoping out the market and doing a thorough SWOT analysis of reclaimed barnwood, along with companies that recover and sell reclaimed barnwood, they discovered some significant weaknesses their competitors face. Reclaimed barnwood has many shortcomings. It is old wood from barns, meaning it's often brittle and inconsistent in size, color, and dimensions, making it hard to work with. It can also contain toxins, insects, and animal waste and smells from barn animals. It is also expensive. They found some reviews online from builders and contractors and even contacted a few interior designers directly. They learned that there is disappointment and frustration in many aspects of the process, including in acquiring samples, slow response times to inquiries for product information and pricing, quantities available in specific colors, and inconsistent lead times.

Everything they learned led them to believe their new idea could be a better solution. Tim was an innovator, a bit of a "mad scientist," and he developed a new type of barnwood that is purposefully made—a real wood product made to look like old, reclaimed barnwood. It is made with a consistent color finish in the most popular colors and machined to exact specifications and lengths, making it easy to work with and predictable in quantities needed for specific jobs.

Mike had worked as a carpenter as a young man and spent most of his career in the construction industry. His passion and focus were on how they could offer a different and better customer experience. After learning about the many customer service frustrations in the industry, he believed they could figure out how to improve the experience and make it so much better and easier for customers. Then they could offer a better product and better service.

Mike and Tim also learned from their market analysis using ZoomInfo that while many companies offer reclaimed barnwood for sale, most are small companies in terms of sales revenue and primarily sell their products regionally rather than shipping them all over the country. Finding competitor pricing proved to be easy, as many of the companies included pricing on their websites.

Confident and excited about what they had learned in their market analysis, Mike and Tim began to develop their strategy around their unique identity (market position) and to create an initial draft of their CVP. Here's what it looked like:

- Provide world-class, market-leading customer service to every influencer in the process, from design to buying decision to delivery.

- Streamline the supply chain and order-to-delivery process, and ship project orders directly from our warehouse to any job site in the country within five to seven business days.

- Ship samples the same day upon request by anyone involved in the project, at no charge.

- We will be an expert resource on any and all questions related to product specifications, project design, and installation.

- Ship orders complete and deliver on time to customers.

- **CVP: We will provide the best products, the best price, and the best service for our customers.**

We will revisit Mike and Tim in the Hack in Action in Hack 6 to show how they transformed their customer value proposition into setting the goals and success standards to drive their actions and measure their performance.

The John Savage quote at the beginning of this Hack gave you a clear perspective on how to approach your market analysis and develop your customer value proposition. In Hack 1, we started with the basics of defining the problem and outlining your potential solution. Completing a comprehensive market analysis is a crash course in getting vested in the industry and the market through research and discovery, and it further ignites your passion and motivation to carry your idea and solution through to the next steps to launch your new business.

Throughout my career, I have been conditioned to start with the consumer and work my way backward when determining how products or services can be different and better, formulating a written customer value proposition. We refer to the end customer as the "ultimate decision-maker." If it works for them, it is much easier to see how it will work for other influencers in the buying process.

Today's advanced tools and resources can provide remarkable data-driven intelligence to support sound business decisions. Applying traditional tools and the ever-evolving advanced tools will support an effective framework for your market research to develop your best possible solution.

For example, emerging artificial intelligence (AI) tools

are pushing the limits of what is possible in every business area. AI allows entrepreneurs and companies to respond more quickly to market demands. In product development, AI enhances the efficiency and speed at which products can be effectively developed, addressing variables such as innovative design, supply chain optimization, quality assurance, project management, data-driven predictions of market trends, and a deeper understanding of end customer behaviors.

We all have a compass within us, and as eager entrepreneurs with strong convictions in our solutions, objective analysis and learning are key elements to our success. Combining traditional and advanced market analysis tools and methods, coupled with strategic thinking and interpretation, gives you a comprehensive understanding of your competitive landscape and offers guidance as you develop your best solution and customer value proposition.

The next page shows a checklist to help you stay organized with your progress.

HACK 2
LAY A SOLID FOUNDATION

Completed

Have you completed a SWOT analysis for two to three direct competitors? ☐

Have you built competitor files and acquired product and marketing samples? ☐

Have you developed a rough draft of your CVP? ☐

Are you prepared to move to the next phase of construction? ☐

HACK 3

BREAK GROUND AND CLAIM YOUR SPACE

Define Your Identity and Make It Yours

An institution is the lengthened shadow of one man [person].

— RALPH WALDO EMERSON, ESSAYIST AND PHILOSOPHER

THE PROBLEM: WE HAVE ONE CHANCE TO MAKE A FIRST IMPRESSION

THE CONSTRUCTION WORLD includes many trade-contracting businesses, such as plumbers, electricians, carpenters, roofers, siders, insulators, flooring installers, and painters. Imagine you are looking for a specific type of carpenter who can do intricate finish work in your home. You start with an online search to find a carpenter who offers detailed finished woodworking. The search results are an endless list of carpenters in the area, and at first glance, they all look the same. Most company names seem to be the owner's name with the word "carpentry" after it. The owner's name means nothing to you because you don't know them, and the word carpentry is vague. You're just trying to find the service you need with some initial confidence in the company and service you are looking for. Frustration may quickly set in after you visit a few websites and call a couple of them. Without any detail on their specialty and with only their name to go on, you decide you will not waste your time if the company names don't offer some initial perception about what they do.

Your company name is the initial contact point for potential customers. With so many business options readily available, if you don't make a lightning-fast and meaningful connection with potential customers, your startup can be lost in the crowd. If your company name is not memorable and does not resonate by quickly and effectively describing your product or service, then it will be more difficult to effectively gain customers and grow your business. If potential customers are not motivated to learn more about your business and what you can do for them, they will move on to another company that they believe will be more likely to meet their needs.

The lack of a meaningful name for your new business can compromise your one chance to make a good first impression and fail to help you connect with your target audience. This can result in higher costs to effectively market and promote your product or service and gain new customers.

THE HACK: BREAK GROUND AND CLAIM YOUR SPACE

Naming your business should be a fun and exciting process. Think about the pride you feel, what it means, what it represents, your brand identity and logo, your company colors, marketing opportunities, and the confidence it will instill in anyone who decides to interact and do business with your company.

Choosing the right name for your startup has significant benefits. It conveys professionalism and establishes credibility. A distinctive name can make it easier for gained customers to refer your business to others, expanding your marketing reach. It also stands out from competitors in online searches. You can see that the company name has a lasting impact on the long-term growth potential of your new business.

WHAT YOU CAN DO TOMORROW

Choosing a name for your business can feel as exciting as the initial lightning bolt of inspiration that led you to start your business. Harness that excitement but temper it with a practical edge that will help you gather a team, examine your options, and choose a name for your product or service that will give you staying power in a competitive business world.

- **Identify the participants in the process.** Assemble a diverse team that will approach the process by utilizing their unique talents, experience, and perspectives. Examples include business colleagues, potential customers, and influencers such as a trusted friend who knows you well and has no vested interest in the business or history in the market or industry. The business owners will ultimately decide on the company name, but they would be wise to get varying perspectives so they can make the best decision on a meaningful name.

- **Put your CVP to work.** Let's go back to the initial draft of your customer value proposition, describing the unique benefits your company promises to deliver to its customers. It articulates why the customer should buy a product or service from your company and what makes you the best choice. It's time to put it to work to establish your business name and identity. Use your CVP to guide and inspire you as you begin the eight-step process (in the next section) for naming your business. You can use your written CVP to communicate your vision effectively and consistently with the team you assemble to participate in the business-naming process.

- **Capture thoughts and details in writing.** Like any effective business meeting with multiple participants, begin with an agenda and your desired outcomes or goals. Capturing details, discussions, and outcomes in writing helps the group quickly pick up where a decision was made to move to the next step. Using a whiteboard or digital notes on a monitor in real time is an excellent way to capture thoughts visually, collaborate, and maintain group focus.

- **Make it relevant.** Starting a business is expensive, so you'll want to get the maximum value from your name and messaging. A relevant business name generates the initial connection with your target audience. Avoid hard-to-spell names, wordy names, play-on-words names, words that are hard for your target market to pronounce, and names that try too hard to be catchy or rhyme. I am a big proponent of not including owner, family, or dedication names when naming a business. Make the words meaningful and relevant to the product or service, not to potential owners. Your business is much more likely to capture a customer's attention when your business name aptly describes the product or service the customer is looking for.

BUILDING MOMENTUM

The first four recommendations in the previous section are a stellar start to establishing the framework for the critical task of naming your business. Here, we go into a more detailed eight-step strategic process to help you create an effective and valuable name for your startup.

STEP 1: Reflect on what you want to project.

Think about your values, your business purpose, and the initial impression of your business that you want to convey. Capture these thoughts in a few sentences and write them down. Also, keep your written CVP front and center to guide you.

STEP 2: Research other business names in your industry.

You want your business name to stand out, so this process will give you valuable data about names, terms, and phrases you may want to avoid. It can also provide relevant themes in your product or service market and generate creative ideas and direction. The goal is to be unique and stand out while staying within the relevant, common understanding of your industry and business type.

STEP 3: Brainstorm potential names.

Brainstorm a list of names with keywords related to your industry and market and reflecting the unique characteristics of your business. Online brainstorming tools can help. I advocate keeping this simple and allowing creative thought to drive the process. I recommend a simple and effective tool: an online thesaurus. These resources offer synonyms and their definitions. Considering related word options can enhance your creativity and offer ideas for additional precise word choices.

STEP 4: Gain first-impression reactions from others.

Identify a select group of friends, family, and trusted business colleagues who will share their first-impression reactions to your potential business names. This group should be brutally honest in sharing their input. Here are a few questions you can ask them for more targeted feedback:

- *First impressions:* What is your immediate reaction? What thoughts or feelings does it evoke?

- *Relevance:* Does the name convey what the business does or offers?

- *Memorable:* Is the name easy to remember?

- *Uniqueness:* Does the name stand out from competitors?

- *Pronunciation and spelling:* Is the name easy to pronounce and spell?

- *Market fit:* Does the name fit the target audience and industry?

- *Longevity:* Do you think the name will be relevant in five to ten years?

- *Call to action:* Would you be more inclined to learn about or engage with a business with this name? Why or why not?

STEP 5: Check availability.

Conduct an online Google search for potential domain name availability to determine if another business already uses the name. The sites domain.com and godaddy.com are fairly quick and easy to use and offer close alternatives if your specific domain name is taken. If you have researched business names in your industry and worked through an effective brainstorming process, odds are you will find relevant business names that are already taken or close to your potential company name. At this point, consider several names as options as you work your way through the rest of the process.

STEP 6: Visualize the name.

Envision each name represented in different mediums, such as print marketing materials like letterhead, business cards, and brochures; digitally on your website and social media platforms; signs on an office or storefront; and even how it may look on wearables, a vehicle, or a billboard. With all the different channels for showing your company name, finding consistency and quality is the goal. Short and simple is better. Avoid names that are difficult to pronounce or include a complicated meaning that is not easily understood or relatable to your product or service. A good example for a roofing contracting business would be Weatherproof Roofing. It's simple, easy to understand, and instantly relatable to what the business does. A less effective example would be KJT Services. Even if KJT is the owner's initials and therefore connected to the person providing the service, they are unknown to potential customers. Furthermore, "Services" is too vague and does not identify the business's product or service.

STEP 7: Think about the future.

How will your name accommodate future growth and changes in your business? We cannot predict the future, but we can think strategically about potential expansion, growth, and how the business could evolve with new products and service offerings. If you have a new solution that is truly new, different, and better, work on developing a business name and focus on that single potential "game changer" to realize the full market advantage now. A future marketing strategy involves using marketing taglines, which you can use to promote your business and inform customers about new product offerings and enhanced services. A marketing tagline is a memorable statement or motto that accompanies and reinforces your company name and brand. Its purpose is to enhance or express a company's greater purpose and mission, and it can also broaden customers' perspectives of your business beyond your business name.

Nail It:

Agree to set aside logo design until later. It is easy to get caught up in the creative process of developing a new business name. It is helpful to visualize the potential look of your business name and brand mark as a first step. However, resist the temptation to work toward finalizing your graphics, logos, taglines, and colors. In Hack 8, we will spend more time developing a marketing plan and finalizing the elements that will become your brand's visuals.

STEP 8: Decide on it.

It's time to assess all your research, data, and team opinions from these steps and choose your business name. It's almost time to purchase the all-important domain name to go with it.

REMOVING OBSTACLES

Deciding on a name for your startup is a subjective process that can leave you wondering whether you are making the best decision. Setbacks and roadblocks may hinder the process and cause you to feel frustrated, leading to decision fatigue. Here are a few common obstacles you may experience in naming your business, along with solutions for working through them.

How do I know if we have landed on the best name? If you have done your homework and followed the process with a pragmatic business approach, then you can feel confident that you have done your best and that your business name will project confidence to your potential customers. Also, keep in mind that your business name is the first interaction with customers, and you will have many more interactions that will represent your company, build equity, and establish your brand value over time.

What if the team does not agree on the name? A lack of consensus can be tricky, especially if you have multiple owners who disagree. If you worked through the eight-step process, you likely chose a name (or narrowed the list down to two or three). If you are having trouble reaching a consensus or making that final decision, you might want to invest in a consultation with a marketing brand expert or organize a small focus group to share the pros and cons of the potential names.

What if the domain name is taken? If you have decided on the perfect business name that meets all the criteria throughout the naming process, but the domain name is not available, here are some options for you to consider:

- Use a synonym tool, such as thesaurus.com, to generate relevant alternative words for your business name, then search for available domain names with the new options.

- Domain names contain two components: the name (the part you create) and the suffix at the end, known as the TLD (top-level domain), such as .com. The TLD .com is the most common and popular. However, consider other TLD options such as .net, .co, .tech, .food, .diy, and country-specific suffixes such as .us or .uk.

- You may be able to purchase domain names that someone already owns. Some individuals buy popular domain names to make a profit. The domain name may not be active with a live website, and the owner is just looking to sell it. There are also active domain names available for purchase, and you might have the option of contacting the owner with an offer to buy the domain name. Both are viable options depending on how much you decide is reasonable to pay for your ideal domain name.

What if we are not creative? I can relate. Few people would describe me as creative. No one would look to enlist my "elite skills" in brand development. However, by recognizing this about myself, I have benefited by seeking creative expertise from others on many past projects. A wealth of freelance creative thinkers are out there. Simply conduct an online search for a freelance brand strategist or freelance consultant to name your business. Freelance consultants are plentiful and affordable. You can review their work, experience, and perspective and even interview them to find the right person to include as a participant in the naming process.

Should I consider using owner names or initials in our company name? You'll want to consider these questions when deciding whether you should include the owner's name or initials in the company name:

- *Am I the product or service?* If you are the only employee and your specific output or expertise is the product or service—for example, a consultant or interior designer—you may include your name as part of the company name. But if your business grows beyond the individual, you might regret the limitations of tying the business to a specific person or family.

- *Would the name connect with my target audience?* The owner's name in the business name will only connect with your target audience if the business owner(s) is well-established and recognized in the industry or market and will enhance confidence, foster a positive professional perception, and connect emotionally with your target audience.

- *Could we sell the business in the future by using a family name?* My recommendation is that if you think you will potentially sell your interest in the business in the future, do not include any owner names in the company name. The company name will be less valuable to a potential buyer if you are no longer an owner. Focus on a relevant business name that does not include individual or family names.

Should I consider trademark protection for our company name? Think of a trademark as a legal means of protection to differentiate your company name from competitors or other companies. Different elements of businesses can be trademarked: the name of the company, the name of a specific product, design marks such as logos or symbols, or a combination of these representative elements. Trademarking your business name is a proactive step in establishing your unique business identity. If you decide to pursue trademark protection, I recommend you consult with legal counsel specializing in trademark and patent law to conduct a basic search. There is typically a reasonable fixed package cost for a trademark search and analysis, so confirm the cost and the details provided in the search result. As you build your brand presence, it becomes a more valuable and long-term asset you may want to protect.

THE HACK IN ACTION

Jennifer and Beth decided to open a new business to provide pet grooming care, pet boarding, and pet sitting. Both are animal lovers, see their pets as family members, and have experienced poor service from pet care providers. They believe it can and should be done better.

Their services will include pet grooming and pet care when customers are working or traveling. Their customer value proposition is about caring and convenience: caring for pets with the unparalleled convenience of on-site pet boarding, in-home pet sitting, or a combination of both to make the experience flexible, easy, enjoyable, and stress-free for furry family members. Premium grooming services will also be available on-site or in the home. They anticipate that most of their business will be taking care of dogs, since dogs need regular daily care and socialization, but they will also provide in-home care for cats, birds, and other small pets.

The process for naming their business was disappointing at first. Jennifer and Beth quickly came up with two company names that they agreed would be good options: Dog Daze and Canine Concierge. They were confident that either business name would be a fine choice to represent their customer value proposition. However, a Google search revealed a similar company named Dog Daze in their state less than sixty miles away. A GoDaddy search showed that the domain name dogdaze.com was available, but with the business name already in use and close to their market service area, they decided to eliminate it as an option.

In their Google search for Canine Concierge, they found a company with a similar name offering similar services located over seven hundred miles away in another state.

They also found that if they chose the name, they could acquire the domain name canine-concierge.com, but further online research revealed that those words were broadly used in pet care with varying services. They even found a nonprofit organization using the same name. Jennifer and Beth decided to start over, searching for a business name that was unique, relevant to their business, and conveyed their love of dogs. Beth captured their brainstorming session on a whiteboard to visualize the names and track their progress. See the following list of potential names.

The list of names provided good visual comparisons, and after discussion and debate, they agreed that Dog's Best Friend was unique and relevant to "man's best friend." They felt it represented their love of dogs and communicated how much they care for animals.

Potential company names:

Dog Daze
Canine Concierge
JBM Pet Services
Pet Sitters
Dog Sitters
Man's Best Friend
Dog's Best Friend
Dog Friendly
Pet Attendants
Pet Pals
Doggie Daycare

A Google search was positive, too. They couldn't find any businesses named Dog's Best Friend, and search results showed the many reasons dogs make the best friends. They conducted a domain search and found that the dogsbestfriend.com domain was owned but had no active website. They could purchase dogsbestfriend.com for $69.99 from a seller through the GoDaddy site. GoDaddy suggested an alternative domain, dogs-bestfriend.com, so they decided to purchase and register both domain names. This was a strategic decision because they figured they would use the primary website domain address and own the alternative to prevent someone else from registering and owning it. Jennifer and Beth agreed to invest in a trademark search with a trademark and patent attorney and found that A Dog's Best Friend had been trademarked years ago for a dog chew toy product, but the trademark had expired. Considering the uniqueness of the name and their future investment in marketing, advertising, and building their brand, they decided to work with their attorney to trademark register Dog's Best Friend once they finalized the visual design of their name and logo.

A *Forbes* article, "Eight Common Reasons Small Businesses Fail," published in October 2019, reported that 20 percent of small businesses fail in the first year, 30 percent in the second year, and 50 percent by the fifth year. Two of the most common reasons small businesses struggle and potentially fail are unsuccessful marketing initiatives and a lack of an effective, aligned, and dedicated management team.

In today's world, when we want something, we immediately conduct an internet search for it, and numerous competing options appear. A relevant and meaningful company name, including search words that your ideal customer will use and associate with your brand, is essential for success. Startups typically have limited marketing funds, so creating a relevant and meaningful name that directly communicates your product or service is a cost-effective way to communicate what your company does in every marketing initiative and customer interaction. Get the most out of your company name.

Use the following checklist to help you stay organized with your progress.

HACK 3
BREAK GROUND AND CLAIM YOUR SPACE

Completed

Have you identified the key participants in the naming process? ☐

Have you worked through each of the eight steps for naming your business? ☐

Did you purchase and register a domain name? ☐

Are you prepared to move to the next phase of construction? ☐

HACK 4

MAKE IT OFFICIAL
Choose the Best Legal Structure

*You can't build a great building
on a weak foundation.*

— GORDON B. HINCKLEY, RELIGIOUS LEADER AND AUTHOR

THE PROBLEM: THE WRONG
LEGAL STRUCTURE IS COSTLY

ARCHITECTS AND BUILDERS must follow state and local building codes to be legally compliant during the construction process. Failure to follow building codes or acquire the proper permits can lead to unnecessary legal, financial, safety, and even resale risks. The penalties for not following the rules can be substantial and range from small fines for minor violations to severe penalties for more substantial violations that escalate during the duration of non-compliance.

Imagine if your builder did not follow state and local building codes, pull the proper permits, or comply with the inspections during the construction process. You would likely experience construction delays with stop work orders, financial problems, increased costs, appraisal issues with your mortgage lender, and future resale complications in having to bring violations up to the current code, delaying the sale and increasing your costs.

Like building a home, starting a business requires following the rules and being in legal compliance. Choosing the wrong legal structure can bring unnecessary legal, tax, liability, and decision-making risks to your business and you as the owner. Most startup owners are not licensed attorneys, tax specialists, or certified public accountants. Without the proper legal structure, your startup may fail before it even begins, and not partnering with a trusted expert can expose your new business to significant risks. The risks include:

- *Legal liability:* If the business doesn't have the appropriate legal structure, you could be personally liable for business debts and legal claims.

- *Tax issues:* Improper structuring can lead to unexpected or higher tax obligations.

- *Compliance violations:* Failure to comply with federal, state, or local regulations can result in legal actions or even force you to close your business.

- *Business dissolution risks:* The lack of a well-structured operating agreement can result in partnership disagreements, potentially leading to the dissolution of the business.

- *Funding and investment issues:* If the business doesn't have a strong legal structure that minimizes risks, investors are less likely to invest in your business.

- *Intellectual property (IP) risks:* Failing to adequately protect your brand, ideas, or products with trademark and patent protections could leave you vulnerable to theft, compromising your competitive advantages.

THE HACK: MAKE IT OFFICIAL

The legal structure of your new business defines the organizational and ownership structure. There are several legal business structures for startups, all with pros and cons, so you will want to choose carefully. To simplify, we will work through the process referred to as the "Five-for-Five Method." There are five main types of business structures for startups and five key considerations to determine the best legal structure for your new business. You can see the breakdown in Table 4.1.

Five-for-Five Method

The Five Considerations	The Five Legal Structures
Flexibility and scalability	Sole proprietorship
Complexity	C corporation (C corp)
Liability protection	Limited liability company (LLC)
Tax implications	S corporation (S corp)
Management structure	Partnership

Table 4.1

THE FIVE CONSIDERATIONS

1. Flexibility and scalability refer to the ease and potential to change your business structure in the future if needed or if there are benefits or tax advantages to making a legal structure change. Your new business may be simple at the start, and the legal structure may also be simple. However, as your business evolves, grows, and experiences changes, such as new investors, a partner, personal life changes for you as the owner, succession planning, or any other positive or negative impacts on your business, it is essential to consider future possibilities. Simply put, flexibility allows you to adapt successfully.

2. Complexity refers to the intricacies of different legal structures. While legal structures may seem straightforward, there are layers of administrative complexities that require legal filings and have tax implications. Complexity comes with the costs of time and money invested in processes and fees. Another element of complexity involves the timeliness of annual legal filings and requirements. The government does not make the compliance requirements for administration easy to navigate. Legality and complexity go hand in hand; unfortunately, the government and "easy" do not.

3. Liability protection refers to the scope of legal responsibility with more legal considerations and implications. Are you seeing a trend here? The goal in deciding on your legal business structure should be to limit the personal liability you are responsible for and separate your personal assets from your business responsibilities. Doing the right thing is paramount and a priority for any well-intended business owner, but navigating legal responsibility between personal and professional is critical, not just at the start of your business entity but also on an ongoing basis as your business changes over time.

4. Tax implications refers to the ever-changing tax laws and liabilities that financially impact your business. The goal with tax implications should be to minimize, minimize, minimize your tax liability when you start your business while simultaneously meeting all the compliance requirements of your legal business structure. This is not to imply that you solely choose your business structure based on this consideration but to minimize your tax liability at the start. Consider your need for flexibility in future considerations, balancing your personal and business tax liabilities.

5. Management structure determines how the roles, hierarchy of authority, and responsibilities will be assigned, controlled, and coordinated. It also impacts the content and flow of shared information. If you have more than one owner or stakeholder with a financial investment in the business, this will be part of the consideration when you choose the legal business structure that makes the most sense for your new company.

THE FIVE LEGAL STRUCTURES

1. Sole proprietorship. As the name implies, a sole proprietorship is a business owned and operated by one person. Sole proprietorships are popular when one person is the only employee; for example, a writer, graphic designer, home cleaner, handyman, childcare provider, tutor, or music teacher … you get the idea. The management structure is simple, and taxes are typically filed with the owner's personal tax return.

Pros

- *Inexpensive.* As the most straightforward form of a business, a sole proprietorship is low-cost to set up with minimal fees, paperwork to file, and little or no applicable regulations.

- *Tax deduction benefits from being self-employed.* Benefits may include health insurance premium deductions and permissible deductions of social security and healthcare expenses.

- *Complete control and privacy.* As the sole proprietor, you have the authority over all business decisions, and you are not required to file annual reports with state or federal governments, avoiding public disclosure of your business information.

Cons

- *Personal liability.* The owner is personally responsible for the company's debts and liabilities, putting their personal assets at risk.

- *Life change limits.* If the owner dies, the business, along with its assets and liabilities, becomes part of the owner's estate, potentially negatively impacting the estate, which will be financially responsible for any outstanding liabilities (debts).

2. C Corporation. A C corporation is a separate legal entity from the business owners and protects the owners from personal liability. It is a common structure when there are two or more owners and ownership shares will be issued, typically based on the percentage of ownership or investment in the business. A business that becomes a corporation is described in legal terms as "incorporated" with the suffix "Inc." included in the business name. Incorporation is the process of writing up a document known as articles of incorporation and itemizing the company's shareholders.

Pros

- *Flexibility and business continuity.* Ownership is easy to transfer with the existence of ownership shares to potential beneficiaries. Also, there are no limits to the number of shareholders that can be added through new owner investment. Business continuity is gained through the percentage of stock held, so the business can run without disruption, even if a shareholder leaves or sells their shares.

- *Liability protection.* Owners are not personally liable for a corporation's debts. Personal assets such as investments, bank accounts, and even cars are protected. As an independent entity, a corporation can file and receive lawsuits, but individual investors are not personally or financially liable for legal actions against the corporation.

- *Capital access.* Corporations can raise funds to support the business by selling company stock and offering ownership shares as an employee benefit. In the early stage of a business, this capital can be valuable in a time of need when expenses potentially deplete existing capital and the profit dollars generated by the business.

- *Tax exemptions.* Corporations can deduct certain benefits they provide to employees, such as retirement plans, health insurance premiums, life insurance, and other related expenses. These deductions are a benefit, but this benefit may not

outweigh a potential "double tax" that shareholders could incur.

Cons

- *Complexity and costs.* Flexibility comes at the
  cost of processes and fees to file state paperwork,
  along with fees of incorporation every year.

- *Administration.* Another requirement of a corporation is to have a board of directors, conduct
  annual shareholder meetings, and file annual
  financial reports with applicable state and other
  potential governmental regulators.

- *Double tax.* Owners (shareholders) pay what
  is referred to as a double tax rather than pass-
  through taxation in a sole proprietorship. This
  means that any profit distributions to shareholders are subject to applicable federal, state,
  and local taxes separately in the form of income.

3. Limited liability company (LLC). A limited
liability business structure limits the personal financial liability to the investment in the company made
by the individual members. LLCs have been referred
to as "hybrid" business structures because they combine the asset protection of a corporation with the tax
characteristics and simplicity of a sole proprietorship or
partnership.

Pros

- *Limited liability.* As stated in its name, the personal assets of LLC members are protected from being required to pay off business debts if the business struggles to be financially successful and profitable.

- *Easy to set up.* In most states, you can form an LLC online in just a few minutes by filling out the formal legal document referred to as the articles of organization. Once this is filled out and approved, you are off and running.

- *Tax benefits.* If you are a single-member LLC getting started in your new business, as in a sole proprietorship, you do not have to report your business assets and liabilities on a separate tax return, and you can take advantage of pass-through taxes. Your income or losses from business operations are transferred to your personal tax return, typically using a Schedule C. All profits gained are taxed at your individual tax rate, and LLCs avoid the double-taxation incurred in other legal business structures.

Cons

- *More difficult transfer of ownership.* If you have multiple owners in your business, all owner-members must approve the addition of new members or any changes in the percentage of ownership. This can create difficulty in decision-making and adding additional funding for the business.

- *Record tracking.* LLC owners must maintain their personal records separate from the LLC's records and operations. This includes separate personal and company business funds, bank accounts, and financial transactions and records.

- *Immediate recognition of profits.* LLCs are required to recognize profits as soon as they are earned. For example, if you are a seasonal business and your income is high in those seasonal months, then you may have to pay taxes on profits that have not yet been realized. "Realized" in this context means that you have not paid out profits gained in the higher-income months but rather measure your financial performance over a longer defined business cycle, typically a calendar year or fiscal year.

4. S corporation. An S corporation is often referred to as a "small-business corporation." It is a business structure like an LLC that is permitted to pass its taxable income, credits, deductions, and potential losses directly to its shareholders. It gives certain advantages over the more common C corporation and is only available to small businesses with a small number of owner-shareholders (less than one hundred and only residents of the United States). It is considered an alternative to a limited liability company.

Pros

- *Limited liability.* Similar to an LLC, an S corp offers personal liability protections from paying off business debts if the business struggles to be financially successful and profitable.

- *Tax benefits.* Again, like an LLC, an S corp can file pass-through taxes. Your income or losses from business operations are transferred to your personal tax return. However, there are also corporate tax savings, whereby a business that is registered as an S corp can also benefit from not having to pay federal taxes at the corporate level. Saving money on corporate taxes is beneficial in the early years of the business.

- *Flexible transfer of ownership.* Interests can be transferred or sold to new owners without complicated or expensive tax implications. An S corp can continue as a legal entity past the owner's lifetime, which is an advantage if the owner wants to arrange for a succession plan or sale of the business upon retirement.

Cons

- *Administration.* An S corp has many structural process requirements and tax rules that make it more complicated to operate than a simple sole proprietorship or LLC. Internal requirements include having a board of directors, written corporate bylaws, conducting and recording shareholder meetings, and logging minutes of significant company meetings. Ongoing IRS rules must be addressed regularly to maintain proper compliance to operate as an S corp. Lastly, there are restrictive distribution rules where the allocation of profits and losses must be based strictly on the percentage of ownership or the number of shares each individual holds.

- *Complex setup process.* Properly setting up an S corp requires time and money. The business owner must submit articles of incorporation with the secretary of state in the state where the company is based. Many states require an annual report fee, franchise tax, and other fees specific to the state. There are also IRS setup requirements, such as being incorporated in the United States, having only one class of stock, having a limited number of shareholders, and being subject to approval for the status to operate as an S corp.

- *IRS scrutiny.* S corp owners who perform more than just minor work for the business typically need to be on the payroll because they must pay themselves a reasonable salary. The IRS scrutinizes how S corps pay their employees because S corps can disguise salaries as corporate distributions to avoid paying payroll taxes. An S corp must pay reasonable salaries to shareholder-employees for services rendered *before* making any distributions. The tax advantages of an S corp make it more vulnerable to IRS tax audits. Accurate bookkeeping is critical.

5. Partnership. In a partnership business structure, two or more people own and operate the business. It is one of the simpler choices of a legal business structure when there is more than one owner. There are two types of partnerships: *general* and *limited.* In a general partnership, owners have equal roles in owning and operating the company, along with its financial obligations and the actions of the other partners. A limited partnership includes both general and limited partners. The general partners have the same roles and liabilities as in a general partnership. The limited partners are typically investors and have more passive ownership roles with limited authority or input on the company's operation. Limited partners do benefit from limited or no liability.

Pros

- *Simple startup.* Setting up a partnership as a legal business structure does not require filing paperwork with the federal government. Filing paperwork as a partnership varies at the state level, but if it is required, it is generally a simple process.

- *Tax benefits.* A partnership legal business structure does not pay tax on its income, so there is no need to file business tax returns. Like a sole proprietorship or limited liability company, you can take advantage of pass-through taxes, filing income or losses from business operations on your personal tax return.

- *Combined knowledge.* Two heads can be better than one. Having a partner with different strengths, skills, and expertise can be valuable. A different perspective can also be a competitive advantage as the business faces challenges as it evolves and grows.

- *Shared finances.* Having a co-owner can reduce the financial burden of starting the company. Also, banks are more likely to offer loans to multi-owner businesses with a shared risk, and banks can help in the early stages of financing the business.

Cons

- *Personal liability.* Similar to how it works in a sole proprietorship, a partnership's owners are personally responsible for the company's debts and liabilities, putting their personal assets at risk. However, limited partner responsibility is limited to their investment in the business.

- *Decision-making.* One pitfall of a partnership is that there is no requirement for a formal management structure. Differences of opinion are inevitable and can lead to conflict, struggles for consensus, and a lack of trust. A written operating agreement between the partners is an option to address roles and rules related to decision-making. Defining management roles, the allocation of responsibilities and duties, an authority hierarchy based on ownership and other factors such as expertise, and provisions for changes in the partnership structure can streamline effective decision-making processes. While operating agreements may offer a legal written framework for the decision-making process, they are only as effective as each partner's commitment to adhering to the rules of the agreement.

WHAT YOU CAN DO TOMORROW

- **Find trusted legal counsel.** "Know-how" will always win over "guess-how." Considering the requirements and rules of operation under each of the five legal structures, it is a must to work with a qualified attorney specializing in legal business structures and with experience in drafting complementing operating agreements if your startup has multiple owners.

- **Keep it simple.** If you are the only owner of your new business, there is much less complication since you are the sole decision-maker. All the risks, responsibilities, and liabilities will fall on you, so keep it simple, prioritize tax benefits, and limit your personal liability. You still must think through the considerations and review your legal structure options. However, for many solely-owned businesses, starting as an LLC with an easy setup, personal liability protection, and tax benefits is a good choice.

- **Outline your management structure.** If you have more than one investor in your business, you will have more than one owner and, therefore, more than one decision-maker. Identifying individual owners' levels of investment (percentage of ownership) and their desired level of active involvement in the business can help you form your management team and eliminate legal structures early in the consideration process. To get started in the Five-for-Five Method for your new business, outline your potential management structure. Include details such as each individual's area of expertise, authority level, list of functional responsibilities, and deliverables that contribute to the growth and success of the business.

BUILDING MOMENTUM

Let's accelerate the process and consider the future, understand the dynamics of operating agreements, and finalize your legal structure to officially register your new business.

STEP 1: Answer the question, "Where do I see the business in three years?"

Now that you have outlined your management structure, think and talk openly as owners about where each of you sees the business in three years. Many thoughts and

Make It Official

perspectives are typically shared when considering this question. An owner may want their initial investment back in the short term, they may want to grow the business to sell their interest within three years, or they may want to expand and increase the investment in the business to position it for significant growth beyond three years. Addressing this question openly and candidly as owners will help you select the right legal structure to start your new business.

STEP 2: Compose an operating agreement.

The concern in selecting the best legal structure is more prevalent when there are multiple owners and decision-makers. A good way to address this concern is to include a written operating agreement that complements the selected legal structure. Even though owners have verbally agreed to the terms, duties, responsibilities, and how the business will be run, it is a good practice to create a written operating agreement to govern how the business is run and how decisions are made. A quality operating agreement can provide clarity and alignment for the owners in managing all critical areas of the business and effectively resolving conflicts.

STEP 3: Select your legal structure and register your business.

Now that you've finalized the name for your business and selected your legal structure, the next step is to register the business name with the relevant legal authorities. Most new small businesses only need to register the name with

93

state and local governments. Most small businesses are not required to file with the federal government to become a legal entity other than a simple filing to acquire a federal tax identification number.

REMOVING OBSTACLES

Choosing the best legal structure for your business involves overcoming common hurdles, especially during the startup phase. Here are a few typical obstacles and how to address them.

What if we do not have a consensus on the operating agreement? With multiple owners and stakeholders, you must collectively reach alignment on the roles, rules, responsibilities, and decision-making process in the operating agreement. There will be conflicts, and ultimately, the business will struggle if all owners are not aligned and do not support the operating agreement. If you do not have alignment, the only option is to revisit all aspects of the agreement and commit time to collectively, openly, and honestly discuss concerns to reach a consensus on the necessary changes. If you cannot gain alignment on the operating agreement, then you should not be moving forward with your new business until you do.

Can I change the legal structure of my business in the future? The selected legal structure for your new business does not have to be permanent. I've laid out the five legal structures to invoke strategic thinking as you select the best legal structure to get your business started. Change is inevitable as your new business develops and grows, and changing your legal structure later may be simple or complex. For smaller startup businesses, making a change is easier with fewer stakeholders and simpler operations. However, review these considerations when evaluating a change in your legal structure:

- Size and complexity of your business

- Local or state regulations and filing requirements

- Legal, tax, and operational implications

- Agreement among the owners

- Administrative changes to address (licenses, tax registrations, new employer identification number, updates to bank accounts, new articles of structure to file with the state, and more)

- Effective communication about the change to employees, stakeholders, and perhaps even customers

- Overall cost in time and money versus the benefits of the Five Considerations (flexibility and scalability, complexity, liability protection, tax implications, and management structure)

Isn't it a hassle to reevaluate my legal structure? Review your legal structure annually along with other key business areas. Trigger events during the year may contribute to this annual evaluation. Events such as owners joining or exiting the business, tax changes, funding needs bringing in new stakeholders, new laws or compliance requirements, increased liability protection needs, succession planning, and a change in your business model can warrant a change in your legal structure.

THE HACK IN ACTION

Tom and Pat are friends and have run separate landscape businesses over the past few years. They each have their own trucks, equipment, crews, and books of business to keep their crews busy during the year. Tom has residential contracts primarily in the north end of town, and Pat has residential contracts in the south end. They get together regularly with Joe, a landscape architect, and talk shop about challenges and new opportunities in landscape services. They recently decided to join forces, combining their resources to expand the business into condominium and apartment landscape services, offering landscape design and construction services to their residential customers.

They are all investing an equal amount in the business, and their initial thinking was to form a simple general partnership with equal say and make business decisions based on a majority with three equal owners.

The group decided that Tom and Pat would run the day-to-day business, and Joe would focus on the landscape design service and not be active in the day-to-day operations. However, as an equal investor, he wanted to stay informed and be involved in key decisions. As they discussed roles and responsibilities, they began to question whether a simple general partnership structure would be the best choice.

Since Joe would not be active in the day-to-day business, he expressed concerns over how important topics would be discussed and decisions would be made. Tom and Pat assured Joe that they would keep him informed and suggested that the three of them put together a list of items and topics they should all weigh in on in the decision-making process. Given that Tom and Pat had worked with each other for years and had an established relationship, whereas Joe was a relative newcomer to their group, the three felt that clear guidelines for communication would be best.

They worked through the Five Considerations, deciding to keep things as simple as possible, minimize their liability from their personal lives, and maximize any tax benefits. Working on other people's properties with machinery, Pat and Tom knew from their experience that they would need a robust liability insurance policy for the business. Their insurance provider suggested that they take the liability protection one step further and consider forming a limited liability company that would protect their personal liability and limit business financial liability to their total monetary investment in the business.

As they considered how to form the new company, they liked the benefits of limited liability protection, the ease of setting up an LLC, and the tax benefits. They had already agreed to set up new business accounts under the new company, so recordkeeping and tracking would be manageable. Joe suggested they hire a part-time bookkeeper to manage and administer accounting transactions accurately so Pat and Tom could focus on sales and operations. They agreed it made sense to set up an LLC as the legal structure for the new business.

However, they struggled to gain consensus on one topic. Decision-making still seemed ambiguous to Joe, and while he felt he could trust Tom and Pat, not being active in the day-to-day business was concerning since he worried that as the company grew and they became busy, Tom and Pat might make critical decisions without his input. They agreed that developing a written operating agreement was the right thing to do. They consulted a legal advisor on how to structure the operating agreement to manage the decision-making process effectively, and they learned about many other benefits of having a formal operating agreement. Their finalized operating agreement included a management structure with defined duties and responsibilities, voting and dispute resolution, meeting procedures, how they would manage the tax process and financial matters, and an exit plan if any of them wanted to sell their interest in the new company.

They addressed each of the Five Considerations in their legal structure and were ready to move forward. Tom, Pat, and Joe were excited to use their combined expertise to expand and grow their landscaping services.

Choosing the best legal structure can be stressful and tedious, but it's also incredibly valuable to the owner in both the short and long terms. The goal is to minimize the legal, tax, liability, and decision-making risks and establish a strong foundation for your business.

The Five-for-Five Method (revisit Table 4.1) provides a simple process to follow to compare and contrast the Five Considerations, along with the pros and cons of the Five Legal Structures to decide on the best legal structure for your new business.

If you have more than one owner or stakeholder with a financial investment in the business, and you are selecting the legal structure for your new company, remember these aspects of the process:

- *Communicate*: Share perspectives and concerns openly and honestly.

- *Clarify*: Confirm roles, responsibilities, and authorities in your management structure.

- *Consult*: Talk with a legal expert to review your chosen legal structure.

Use the following checklist to help you stay organized with your progress. Visit the Resources page on ronneary.com to find more downloadable lists.

HACK 4
MAKE IT OFFICIAL

Completed

Have you found and consulted trusted legal counsel? ☐

Did you answer the question: "Where do I see the business in three years?" ☐

Did you select the best legal structure and register your business? ☐

Are you prepared to move to the next phase of construction? ☐

HACK 5

MEASURE TWICE, CUT ONCE
Determine Profit Potential

*Profitability is the only way to
control your own investments.*

— BORJE EKHOLM, CEO OF ERICSSON

THE PROBLEM: NOT CALCULATING PROFIT CAUSES BAD DECISIONS

I N COLLEGE, I worked as a finish carpenter, putting my childhood carpentry skills to work remodeling homes I owned. The phrase "measure twice, cut once" is an old carpentry saying to double-check your measurements for accuracy before cutting a piece of wood. Boy, have I made my share of miscuts over the years. Finish carpentry, as the term states, involves applying finishing touches to complete a home's interior aesthetic and functional elements. It includes detailed cuts, such as installing trim, molding, cabinets, shelves, interior doors, and flooring. Not accurately installing these elements can result in visible gaps and seams, doors that do not properly open and

101

close, unstable cabinets or shelves, warped or loose floor-boards, and weak or loose joints. Ultimately, this causes setbacks in the project, such as increased costs for repairs or replacements, time overruns, and material waste, and it can lower the property value.

Like a finish carpenter who does not double-check his measurements, not calculating the profit potential of your product or service can lead to bad decisions. Poor decision-making on pricing and costs results in cash flow problems where you struggle to pay expenses or get approvals for business loans because you cannot prove or project profit potential. Another problem with the inability to calculate profit is when you focus on the wrong products or areas of your business rather than on the products or areas that are more profitable. Ultimately, not calculating potential profit will lead to business failure in a relatively short time.

THE HACK: MEASURE TWICE, CUT ONCE

To run a successful business, you must make money, whether you want to adequately cover your costs, achieve self-sustainability, or make a big profit. To start, you need to calculate the potential amount of money you can make, called gross profit, for each unit of the product or service you sell. Making money involves determining your gross profit per unit for your product or service and the operating costs you need to run your business.

Begin by calculating an estimate of how much money (gross profit) you make per unit of the product or service.

The calculation will help you answer the following questions: "Am I on the right track?" "Will I make money?" and "Does my new business have a chance of succeeding?"

Determining the overall profit potential of your new business means figuring out how many units of your product or service you need to sell to pay all your expenses and make a profit. Accurately calculating the estimated profit per unit and overall profit potential will help you determine whether you are on the right track to make money and be successful.

WHAT YOU CAN DO TOMORROW

- **Determine your sell price.** In Hack 2, we covered how to research the market and competitors to help you establish a reasonable price range for the sell price of your product or service. If your product or service is similar to a competitor's, then you'll need to price your product or service in a reasonably similar price range. If your product or service is unique with no real comparable product or service available from competitors, then you may decide to charge a higher sell price that reflects the unique value you provide.

For example, let's say you are opening a coffee shop. Your shop may have to charge close to the same amount for black coffee as other shops charge. However, you may offer specialty coffee drinks with a unique taste experience for your customers, and you decide to charge a higher price for those drinks due to the unique value you provide.

- **Identify your unit costs.** List all the items that go into making your product, along with the costs for each item and the labor cost. The total of the items and labor to make each unit is called the "cost of goods sold," or COGS. Labor can be tricky, so keep it simple with the time it would take an employee to make the product.

  Let's continue with the coffee shop example. Break down what you would pay your barista per hour into minutes. The next step would be to multiply the time it takes to make each drink by the amount you would pay the barista per minute. So, for each coffee drink, you will need to list the cost of the coffee beans, cup, lid, other ingredients, and labor. Table 5.1 shows the labor calculation for a caramel macchiato.

Labor cost to make a caramel macchiato

Barista pay/hour	$15.00
Barista pay/minute ($15 / 60 minutes)	$ .25
Time involved	3 min
Total labor cost:	**$ .75**

Table 5.1

Repeat this process for each of the different drinks, adding up the ingredient costs and labor costs to get the total cost of goods sold for each drink. Of course, it would take less time to pour a black coffee, so the labor cost would be less than it is for the caramel macchiato specialty drink.

Let's add up the total COGS for a couple of the coffee drinks in Table 5.2.

Black Coffee	Item Cost	Caramel Macchiato	Item Cost
Cup	$ .15	Cup	$ .15
Lid	$ .10	Lid	$ .10
Coffee	$ 1.00	Coffee	$ 1.00
		Caramel	$ .50
		Whipped cream	$ .40
		Secret ingredient	$ .40
Labor	$ .25 (1 min)	Labor	$ .75 (3 mins)
Total Cost (COGS)	**$ 1.50**	**Total Cost (COGS)**	**$ 3.30**

Table 5.2

- **Calculate gross profit per unit.** Gross profit is the money you make for each unit you sell after subtracting the total costs (COGS) from your sell price.

Gross Profit $ = unit sell price - unit cost

As you get familiar with the different terms, calculations, and financial aspects to measure your startup's performance, you will learn that seeing the calculations in the form of percentages helps you standardize for comparison and supports better strategic decision-making. The gross profit percentage formula involves more than addition and subtraction but is easy to calculate:

Gross Profit % =
(unit sell price - unit cost) / unit sell price

When you work closely with your accountant as you launch and grow your business, you will find that using percentages for comparison is a common financial practice.

Let's continue with the example of the coffee drinks and calculate the gross margin for each:

Black Coffee	Item	Caramel Macchiato	Item
Total Cost (COGS)	$ 1.50	Total Cost (COGS)	$ 3.30
Sell Price	$ 3.65	Sell Price	$ 6.65
Gross Profit $	**$ 2.15**	**Gross Profit $**	**$ 3.35**
Gross Profit %	**59%**	**Gross Profit %**	**50%**

Table 5.3

The sell price for black coffee was determined because it's just black coffee, a
common item available from other local
coffee shops and gas stations. By scoping
out the market, you learned that the sell price
of $3.65 needs to be close to the same size
cup of black coffee from competitors that
also offer black coffee. However, the sell price
for a caramel macchiato is higher because
it's a unique item with a special ingredient
that makes it stand out as different, and you
are sure it's better than other caramel coffee
drinks available at other coffee shops.

• **Estimate and list the monthly costs of operating your business.** Operating costs are
simply the monthly expenses to run your
business. Operating costs include rent,
insurance, salaries, utilities, office supplies,
monthly lease payments for computers

and equipment, maintenance, and other expenses that do not include the direct costs of making the products or services you sell. The simple formula is to list and total all your monthly operating costs. Let's add up the monthly operating costs for the coffee shop example. See Table 5.4.

Item	Monthly Cost
Building rent	$2,000
Coffee machine leases	$ 200
Salaries	$3,800
Insurance	$ 150
Maintenance / other	$ 500
Total Operating Costs Per Month	**$6,650**

Table 5.4

You may wonder why it's important for a business to capture its financial performance in monthly snapshots. Businesses typically measure financial performance in monthly increments largely to ensure regular tax compliance and reporting. Monthly tracking provides timely insights into cash flow, supply costs, sales, gross profits, and operating costs so you can make informed and better business decisions about sell prices and where you may be able to adjust and reduce operating costs to improve your gross profit.

- **Estimate how much you need to sell.** Now, let's pull it all together to figure out how many of your different products you will need to sell each month at a minimum to cover your operating costs. Your goal is not to sell the minimum, of course, but understanding the minimum and the actual sales will help you answer these three questions:

  1. Am I on the right track?
  2. Will I make money?
  3. Does my new business have a chance of succeeding?

  Let's continue with the coffee shop example to figure out how much coffee you need to sell each month to cover your operating costs.

  First, let's simplify the calculations by making these two assumptions for our examples: The coffee shop offers two types of drinks, black coffee and caramel macchiato, and the coffee shop sells the same number of each item per month. (I know it's unrealistic, but bear with me for the clarity of this example.)

Item	Black Coffee	Caramel Macchiato
Sell price for each item	$ 3.65	$ 6.65
Gross margin for each item	$ 2.15	$ 3.35
How many do I have to sell each month?	**1,210**	**1,210**
Monthly sales for each item	$ 4,416.50	$8,046.50
Monthly gross margin for each item	$ 2,601.50	$4,053.50
Total Monthly Sales	$12,463.00	
Total Monthly Gross Margin	$ 6,655.00	
Monthly Operating Costs	($ 6,650.00)	
Monthly Operating Profit	**$ 5.00**	

Table 5.5

As you can see from the example, the monthly gross margin covers the operating costs for the month, with $5 left over as gross profit. Breaking this down even further, adding the quantity of both drinks to sell each month can provide more data to show if you are on the right track and have a chance to be successful. Based on this information, divide the total monthly coffee drinks (2,420) by the

> number of days the coffee shop will be open each month (30), and you can conclude that selling 80 cups of coffee per day will allow you to cover your operating expenses fully. Selling *more* than 80 drinks a day means you start to make money.

BUILDING MOMENTUM

Understanding the different costs and determining your gross profit per unit for your product or service is a great start as you set up your business. Initially, you want to calculate gross profit based on conservative cost and sales estimates.

Now it's time to get creative and see where you can save money, potentially lower individual costs, and maximize your gross profits.

STEP 1: Identify operating costs that you can minimize.

Whether your solution is a product or service, you will inevitably have lower-cost items that make sense to buy in larger quantities. You use these items daily, such as print paper for administrative documentation, napkins and cups for your coffee shop, glass cleaner for your cleaning service, or packaging for your product. However, the key is to understand that while there are positive savings in individual unit costs when buying in larger quantities, you are still tying up cash in your business until your sales volume exhausts the supply of these lower-cost items. Developing your strategic sales plan in Hack 8 will help you choose the quantities to purchase.

STEP 2: Think creatively when negotiating with potential suppliers.

It makes sense to negotiate the cost of an individual item for your business or a component for your product. You can also negotiate other items, including shipping rates, bank rates you will have to pay if you accept customer payments by credit card, and even the payment terms with a supplier you will purchase from regularly. In most cases, when starting a new small business with no sales history or record of being a good-paying customer, there is a limit to the leverage you will have initially. Just as you would in your personal life, do some comparison shopping.

A fair and effective way to get a good price to start with is to be clear that you are considering alternatives and ask potential suppliers to give you their best price. Once you get the comparisons, you can use the best price to negotiate with the supplier you have the most confidence in. Also, be willing to share with your preferred supplier that you are committing to them as your primary supplier if they perform at a high level of quality and service. We will address working with suppliers in more detail in Hack 12.

STEP 3: Build a worksheet to simplify calculations.

Setting up a simple worksheet or spreadsheet with formulas to calculate potential gross profit dollars and the gross profit percentage by item is efficient and accurate. The speed and flexibility of entering values for different costs of items, sell prices, and minimum quantities are an advantage. The worksheet contents foster strategic thinking in how you balance the cost of goods sold (COGS) and operating costs, sell prices, sales quantities, and potential gross profit by item or service. It is also an advantage in Hack 8 when developing marketing and sales plans. If you are not experienced or skilled at creating spreadsheets, I recommend you take a tutorial on the basics or find a friend or colleague who will work with you to set up your calculations.

To get started, go to ronneary.com for a sample spreadsheet you can download.

REMOVING OBSTACLES

Determining your business's profit potential can be arduous and complex. The purpose is to determine whether you are on the right track, can make money, and have a real chance of success. Here are common questions I hear about potential obstacles, followed by my responses.

How will I know if I am capturing accurate costs? You don't know for sure. Hack 5 is about determining profit *potential*. You can get as accurate a picture as possible when you identify the individual costs that will factor into the unit cost for your product or service and the operating costs to run your business each month. Each cost is not permanent, but capturing the closest estimate will help you think strategically to improve and potentially lower different individual costs once you launch and are actively running your business and generating sales.

What if I am unsure whether I have chosen the right sell price? In most cases, customers buy on value and not on price. However, we are all told as buyers that we are getting the best price or that the seller can beat any price. Prices, like costs, are not permanent and move up or down due to changes in the economy, costs, and actions of competitors to adjust their prices up or down, as well as the perception of value you provide to your customers. The key to determining a starting price for your product or service is to find the "reasonable price range" you can charge compared to your direct competitors. The "reasonable range" is an estimate of the low and high prices you discovered during your market analysis in Hack 2.

How do I know if I am getting the best price from my suppliers? As a new business startup, you *will not* get the best price from suppliers. The reality is that they do not have a history with your business. Even if you have a past relationship with a supplier from your industry experience, their relationship with your startup is new. A simple strategy is to ask for price breaks based on the quantity you purchase at one time. The goal is to get your best starting price from your suppliers while being realistic about what you can negotiate. Cost improvement opportunities will come later as you build credibility with your suppliers and prove your value as a reliable customer.

What's the best way to estimate the total number of units I can sell in a month? The unit cost can only be determined by estimating the total number of units you need to sell or produce each month. Think in terms of the quantity you *must sell* to cover your monthly operating costs. This estimate will also help when you get to Hack 7 about managing day-to-day work and creating the operational framework to run your business.

THE HACK IN ACTION

Emily has been making organic soaps for years and prefers natural, organic ingredients and the benefits to her skin. She shared her creations with family and friends as gifts, and when they kept asking her for more, she decided to make her organic soaps into an e-commerce business and sell them online. Now, she makes the organic soaps in a small studio workshop attached to her house. She has all the molds and equipment for measuring, mixing, and heating the soaps, and she has the space for curing, cutting, packaging, and storing.

Emily had one signature soap, Organic Oatmeal, that friends and family have raved about. She decided this would be the organic soap she would start with and believed it to be a sure winner. Her biggest challenge was that she had repeatedly made it as a hobby over the years but had not looked closely at what it would cost to make the soap, package it, ship it, and promote it. Basically, she had not determined whether she could make money by making soap as a side business.

Emily worked with a couple of her ingredient suppliers and learned she could buy the non-perishable ingredients and supplies in larger quantities in bulk packaging, saving her money. That savings would lower her cost per bar and allow her to make more money on the sale of each bar.

She worked through the steps and details to determine her profit potential. First, she scoped out the market to determine a reasonable sell price. From Hack 2, Emily researched and found several premium organic soap products sold online and learned that the retail prices vary from $6 to $14 for a comparable bar of soap. The price range is based on the size of the bar of soap and the ingredients. She decided that $7.95 per six-ounce bar of Organic Oatmeal would be a good starting price. She believed it would offer a good value for the customer and, as an e-commerce business, it would be easy to make price adjustments on her website if needed.

Next, she listed the ingredients, labor, and shipping costs to determine the cost per bar. Emily had made so many Organic Oatmeal bars of soap over the years that she was confident one bar could easily be made and packaged in one minute. She decided she would pay her workers (just one to start) an hourly rate of $18 per hour, calculating a cost of thirty cents to make and package each bar ($18 per hour divided by sixty minutes). Adding up the cost of labor (.30), ingredients ($1.85), packaging (.25), and flat-rate shipping costs ($1.35), she estimated a total cost per bar of $3.75.

Once Emily figured out the cost of making and shipping each Organic Oatmeal bar of soap ($3.75) and decided on a reasonable sell price ($7.95), she calculated that she could make a gross profit of $4.20 per bar on each sale, which was a gross profit of 53 percent.

Emily's monthly operating costs were basic. She saved big by working out of the studio workshop attached to her house and not having to pay rent. She planned to have a part-time hourly employee working thirty hours per week. She also decided not to pay herself for her work until she made a profit.

Emily's monthly operating costs:

Salaries: $2,160
Maintenance/other: $500
Utilities: $200
Insurance: $85
Total: $2,945

Next, she estimated how many six-ounce bars she'd need to sell to cover her monthly costs. Emily calculated that if she sold a minimum of 702 bars per month, she could make just enough monthly operating profit of $2,948.40 to cover her $2,945 in operating costs (see Table 5.6). Operating profit is the profit a business generates from its *main operations* after subtracting operating expenses from gross profit. This measure reflects the efficiency of the company's operations before accounting for interest, taxes, or other non-operating costs.

Organic Oatmeal – six-ounce bar	
Sell price per bar	$ 7.95
Gross margin per bar	$ 4.20
Minimum quantity to sell each month	**702**
Monthly sales	$5,580.90
Monthly gross profit	$2,948.40
Monthly operating costs	($2,945.00)
Monthly operating profit	**$ 3.40**

Table 5.6

Determining the monthly operating profit made Emily excited that she was on the right track to be successful with her e-commerce side business. She thought that in a few months, by adding new customers and repeat buyers, she could make and sell twice the monthly minimum and make a solid monthly operating profit.

Nail It:
Worksheets give you accuracy and flexibility in your calculations.

Emily had a friend who helped her create a simple worksheet where she could enter different quantities and costs, and it would automatically (and accurately) calculate the monthly operating profit (see Table 5.7).

Organic Oatmeal – six-ounce bar	
Sell price per bar	$ 7.95
Gross margin per bar	$ 4.20
GOAL to sell each month	**1,404**
Monthly sales	$11,161.80
Monthly gross profit	$5,896.80
Monthly operating costs	($2,945.00)
Monthly operating profit	**$2,951.80**

SUCCESS!

Table 5.7

Once she reaches the goal of selling twice the minimum and is making money, she plans to add other types of organic soaps and continue to build on her success. Emily felt confident she was on the right track to running a successful startup.

Determining monthly operating profit potential is all about helping you answer these three questions:

1. Am I on the right track?

2. Will I make money?

3. Does my new business have a chance of succeeding?

It's all about the math. Understanding the basic terms and formulas for calculating gross profit for each product or service item, as well as being able to include a breakdown of potential monthly sales estimates and operating profit potential with operating costs, is a critical step in determining whether your business can be successful and make money.

In business terms, this exercise is often called a "pro forma": a projection or forecast of the potential to make money. Estimates, assumptions, and hypothetical scenarios are included in the process to determine whether you are on the right track. I have used this process consistently throughout my career to develop a pro forma and show, with confidence, to myself, owners, teammates, and leaders that we were on the right track with the potential to make money and succeed. I highly recommend this process for its value in helping you answer the same questions for your startup.

Now that you are confident you are on the right track with your new venture, the next step is setting goals and success standards to run a high-performing business with a different and better solution than your competitors.

It may seem like a lot of work, but you are playing it smart by determining your profit potential before you invest more time and money and take on more risk. Measure twice and cut once.

Use the following checklist to help you stay organized with your progress.

HACK 5
MEASURE TWICE, CUT ONCE

Completed

Did you determine your sell price? ☐

Have you determined your unit cost and included estimated labor? ☐

Did you add up your monthly operating costs? ☐

Did you calculate how much you must sell to cover monthly operating costs? ☐

Are you prepared to move to the next phase of construction? ☐

CONSTRUCT A SOLID FRAME
Set Goals and Success Standards

What is not measured cannot be improved.
— WILLIAM THOMSON KELVIN, PHYSICIST AND MATHEMATICIAN

THE PROBLEM: LACK OF DIRECTION CREATES INEFFICIENCY

I N THE CONSTRUCTION world, the structural framing plan is part of the blueprint for building a house. The framing is essential for supporting the structure and the roof, ensuring windows and doors are placed and function properly, connecting the building to the foundation, and integrating the plumbing, electrical, and HVAC systems inside the walls and floors.

If you're building your dream house but the builder had no structural framing plan to follow, the frame would not connect properly to the foundation, and measurements would be incorrect, causing finishing elements such as drywall, windows and doors, cabinets, and the roof not to align or function properly. Also, plumbing, electrical, and HVAC systems would not be routed on the correct pathways. These issues would cause a lack of coordination, communication, and frustration among subcontractors, increased costs from rework, code violations resulting in fines and delays, and structural issues.

A lack of direction in setting goals and success standards in your startup can also create problems, making your business ineffective and unsuccessful. Without goals, your startup will lack cohesive guidance, resulting in poor communication and decision-making, inefficiency, team incoordination, and frustration in not working together and progressing toward the same outcomes. If you do not have standards for measuring your performance, it is impossible to know if you are successful.

THE HACK: CONSTRUCT A SOLID FRAME

Measuring performance is critical to the process of change and improvement. I have worked for and with many companies throughout my career, and the most successful ones measure just about everything. When I thought there wasn't much more they could measure, they would find something else to measure, bringing focus and improvement. We would establish goals and measurables for the overall business down to the individual contributor and every level in between. It often seemed to energize us and become an obsession: *"We can beat that!"*

You cannot measure your company's performance without setting goals. In this Hack, we will explore measurables beyond sales and profitability. Establishing goals and tracking progress toward meeting them shapes your culture and expectations, builds excitement in your business, drives your path to profitability, and fosters a high-performing team that is aligned and focused on common goals.

Goals and success standards are similar, and it makes sense to clarify the differences as you consider what you want to accomplish and how you will measure it. Goals are target outcomes intended to be accomplished in a specific time frame and drive your actions and efforts. They provide vision, direction, and priority to your actions. Success standards measure progress toward specific goals. Think of success standards as a tracking mechanism or tool used to determine whether a goal is being met.

A common framework for goal-setting in business can be applied to your company goals and broken down into individual contributions to support your goals. Think of the acronym SMART, which stands for Specific, Measurable, Achievable, Relevant, and Time-bound. George T. Doran introduced the concept of SMART goals in a 1981 issue of *Management Review*. His article was titled "There's a SMART Way to Write Management's Goals and Objectives." He wrote, "The establishment of objectives and the development of their respective action plans are the most critical steps in a company's management process."

For a new business startup, the SMART method is simple, straightforward, and effective for laying out the longer-term goals for your business and the shorter-term daily goals to maintain your team's focus on what's most important to accomplish each day. See Table 6.1 for more details about SMART goals.

SMART Goals

Specific	**Clearly stated and precise.** The more specific you are, the simpler it will be to develop a plan to achieve it.
Measurable	**Define the criteria for measuring success.** You must be able to quantify the goal to track progress toward meeting the objective.
Achievable	**Be realistic in setting your goals.** It is great to set aspirational goals, but be realistic with what you can deliver based on your skills, resources, and time frame.
Relevant	**Meaningful to your overall priorities.** Think about the functional areas of your business, such as sales, operations, and customer service, and align functional goals that contribute to your overall priorities.
Time-bound	**Set deadlines for achievement.** Deadlines help you establish priorities and a sense of urgency.

Table 6.1

Goal-setting typically involves defining your financial goals of sales and profitability, customer service goals, operational goals, and, depending on your type of business, other specific elements such as safety performance or detailed day-to-day activities that need to be performed flawlessly to support the success of your business.

Working toward your goals involves developing action plans, enlisting your team's accountability, and establishing success standards to monitor progress toward goal achievement in the time frame you choose. For example, setting a long-term goal, such as an annual sales goal, is typically broken down into monthly and quarterly increments to track progress toward meeting the annual goal. Developing sales and marketing plans are specific, long-term examples of actions toward delivering your sales goal. An example of a short-term goal is a daily goal, such as how quickly you respond to customer inquiries. Success standards to monitor and measure progress will support all goals.

Success standards can be objective and subjective. Objective metrics are data-driven and include calculations. Examples include sales quotas, financial metrics such as gross or net profit, return on investment (ROI), revenue per employee (employee productivity rate), and operating cash flows. There are also operational metrics measuring the productivity of activities to run your business. Examples include customer on-time and complete shipments, order fulfillment, lead times, inventory turnover rates, and other activities specific to your business that you want to measure, build on, and improve. Keep them simple to start and expand them as your business grows.

Subjective metrics are closely tied to your vision as an owner and are measured on perception, judgment, and interpretations of employee actions and behaviors. Examples include customer satisfaction surveys, ownership observations, and judgments regarding a culture focused on safety, innovation, continuous improvement, and a sense of urgency.

YOUR SMALL BUSINESS BLUEPRINT

WHAT **YOU** CAN DO TOMORROW

- **Identify customer priorities: What is most important to the customer?** To better understand this, look at items on your product definition checklist, such as customer requirements and your competitive advantages, that you believe will make you different and better. Review your draft customer value proposition and the operational and service activities you will need to perform well to reliably and consistently deliver value to your customers. Reach out to potential customers, and even friends and family members, for their perspectives and feedback.

- **Identify your priorities: What is most important to you and your company?** List what you want to accomplish: sales growth, profitability through effectively controlling price and costs, risk management such as safety and security, financial stability such as maintaining a certain level of cash flow, operational efficiency to manage processes, and resources to scale up and accommodate anticipated growth.

BUILDING MOMENTUM

Now that you have identified the customers and your company priorities, you will want to group them into goals and supporting success metrics using the SMART method. Goals are for the long and short terms. You may have one-time specific goals and ongoing goals you will measure in your daily course of business. Here are the steps to constructing a solid business frame by setting goals and success standards.

STEP 1: Structure your priorities into goals using the SMART method.

A well-articulated goal that is specific about where progress can be monitored and measured is ambitious but reasonable to achieve and is critical for customer satisfaction. A goal that includes a completion deadline is much more likely to be accomplished and to support the success of your business.

Develop a success standard for each goal. Determine how you will measure each goal and if it has a single measure of success (all or nothing) or a range that defines its success (milestones tracking positive progress).

STEP 2: Assign a leader for each goal.

Identify who makes the most sense to be responsible for leading the delivery of a specific goal. If you are the sole owner and only employee, the goals are, of course, your responsibility. If you have multiple owners or, like many

YOUR SMALL BUSINESS BLUEPRINT

new small businesses, a few key employees, assigning a leader for a specific goal is a common way to share responsibilities and enlist accountability.

STEP 3: Track and share.

Track your goal through your success metric to measure your progress. Share the progress regularly with your team during scheduled update meetings, within reports, and in real-time updates on monitors. It is your business, so be creative in what works best for you. I have often used the colors of a traffic light to show how we are tracking toward our goals.

> **RED** – Priority attention to get back on track.
> **YELLOW** – Improvement needed.
> **GREEN** – On track and performing well.

Visuals are an effective way to maintain the focus on priorities, and you may choose another option, such as a thermometer, chart, or graph. Keep it simple and in a format everyone on your team can easily understand. I also recommend holding regular update meetings. The primary benefit is that they are interactive and allow for team input on what is working well or not so well. Sharing thoughts and ideas when discussing how you are doing will naturally lead to action for improvement.

STEP 4: Inspect what you expect.

Subjective success metrics require you to consistently monitor progress. Unlike *objective* success metrics with straightforward calculations, such as a sales report, *subjective* success metrics are often driven by your vision to deliver your unique value, such as the expectation for customer response times. You will need to inspect progress to drive your success standards consistently.

REMOVING OBSTACLES

You can't improve what you can't measure. Setting goals and success standards establishes your initial expectations. You may need to adjust after you launch your business. You may learn that some goals, whether objective or subjective, may be unrealistic. Here is what you can do to address some of those potential obstacles.

What if I am not sure of our limits? I love pushing myself and my teams to achieve goals that seem out of reach, yet the goals still need to be *achievable* (the A in SMART goals). Starting a new business is exciting and consumes a lot of energy, and I am sure you will push yourself and your team to your limits. However, be realistic in your limits and capacity for what you can deliver in your startup goals. Realistic goals result in higher morale, less stress, and consistent motivation to gain traction toward your stated goals.

How can I identify important daily success standards? List the most critical activities you must complete daily to earn business from customers. It can be challenging to consistently convey your vision of how you will be different and better *all day, every day*. Daily activity goals and success standards will help you build your winning culture.

How should I measure subjective goals and success standards for employees? Subjective goals and success standards can be tricky. The assessment measurement is *your* judgment on whether expectations are being met. To be effective and measure progress, provide clear criteria, ask for employee self-assessments, enlist peer reviews for input, and add your observations using specific examples.

What do I do when we reach or don't reach our goals? Some of your initial goals may be too easy, and others too difficult. As you build on your experiences and customer interactions, adjust your goals based on what you learn. Keep them ambitious, but be realistic to maintain focus, motivation, and successful execution. If you decide to adjust your goals up or down, communicate your reasons for making the adjustments and share what you have learned to justify the change.

THE HACK IN ACTION

In Hack 2, Mike and Tim scoped out the reclaimed barnwood market. From their thorough market analysis, they outlined a strategy of their unique identity (market position). They listed the key priorities they felt could make them different and better than competitive businesses that offer comparable-looking wall-covering products.

They crafted an initial draft of their CVP: *We will provide the best products, the best price, and the best service for our customers.*

Mike was a high-energy person who, from his career experience, had developed the habit of doing everything with a sense of urgency. Over the years, he learned that he would need to execute every task related to the business at a high level to deliver on their CVP.

Mike would run the day-to-day business by himself at first, and the plan was to add employees as the business grew. They anticipated a high volume of inquiries from potential customers, and Mike was confident that their processes and tools would provide timely and accurate responses to inquiries. However, he knew that as the business grows and they add new employees, it would be essential to establish goals and success metrics to ensure the team had a clear understanding of day-to-day expectations. He also believed that goals would foster positive energy and a sense of urgency in all their activities and help build an excellent team and culture in their new business. Mike was confident that having clear goals that the team could rally around would provide world-class customer service, driving sales and increasing new customer orders.

He developed the following operational SMART goals and success metrics from the key priorities that would shape their unique identity and help grow their business.

Priority 1: Provide world-class, market-leading customer service to every influencer in the process, from design to buying decision to delivery.

SMART Goal: Return customer inquiries for information and requests for quotes received by phone or email within one hour of being received.

Success Standard:

► Phone inquiries – Using specially made customer service logbooks, record the time the call was taken and whether a request for a quote was given; record the time the formal quote was sent to the customer.

► Email inquiries – Print off quote requests that display the date and time received. Distribute and assign to customer service team members. The team member is to initial for ownership and note the time the formal quote was sent to the customer.

Priority 2: Streamline the supply chain and order-to-delivery process, and ship project orders directly from our warehouse to any job site in the country within five to seven business days.

SMART Goal: Ship all customer orders within twenty-four hours of being received.

Success Standard:

► Using wall job ticket racks with slots displaying each day of the week, insert the customer order details in the slot for the day the order is taken. Once the order is assembled and completed for shipment, the work order is stamped completed with the date and placed in the completed desk file, inspected daily. (Note: This entire process could also take place in a digital platform with shared access, but Mike and Tim chose a manual process at the time.)

Priority 3: Samples will be shipped the same day upon request at no charge, available to all involved in the project.
SMART Goal: Build and maintain a daily inventory of twenty complete sample sets ready for customer shipment, and ship sample sets the same day the customer request for samples is received.

Success Standard:

► Daily visual inspection of the number of sample sets in inventory to ensure that a minimum quantity of twenty is maintained and ready for shipment.

Priority 4: Ship orders complete and deliver on time to customers.
SMART Goal: On-time and complete shipments to customers at a measured rate at or above 95 percent.

Success Standard:

► On-time shipments – Utilize shipping software to monitor confirmed delivery dates.

► Once orders are pulled, a teammate double-checks and initials the accuracy of the order quantities and correct materials to the corresponding work order.

Priority 5: Everyone works safely to ensure we all go home safely with no injuries every day.

SMART Goal: Work safely with zero recordable injuries this calendar year.

Success Standard:

► OSHA (Occupational Safety and Health Administration) will provide our company definition for a recordable injury.

In developing the operational priorities for the business, Mike used the success metrics to provide the tactical, measurable component for each established goal. He also recognized that the measurable components of some goals were objective and easy to calculate the results. Other goals and their corresponding success metrics were subjective and measured based on a timely and regular inspection of progress and results. He established the basic operational service goals and adjusted them as the business grew and changed and when adding employees.

In my career experience working with many types of businesses, from a two-employee company to a larger company with two hundred thousand employees, setting goals and measuring progress are critical to success.

- *Measurement drives behavior:* Measuring performance with clearly stated goals in any business segment drives behavior. This applies to you as well as your employees.

- *Measurement builds your culture:* One more time: *"We can beat that!"* Turning performance measurements into a competition makes the work more exciting and motivating. Whether we are competing against the clock, direct competitors, or each other (in a positive way), the idea of outperforming pushes us to consistently be at our best, collectively reach further for what is possible, and build a solid team and a winning culture.

- *Celebrate your wins when you meet or exceed goals:* Take every chance to celebrate your wins, no matter how big or small. However, strike a balance in how you celebrate to maintain relevance. Celebrating a larger milestone win may be a reason to buy lunch for your team. With a smaller win, a simple team huddle to share the good work and reinforce that you are on the right track with your success standards may be more appropriate.

- *Winning is never final, and losing is never fatal:* Momentum in startup businesses can be fragile. Like momentum shifts in a hockey game, when good and bad things happen, confidence shifts, too. Set goals and success standards that are SMART, drive positive results, and foster a culture of continuous improvement.

Use the following checklist to help you stay organized with your progress.

HACK 6
CONSTRUCT A SOLID FRAME

Completed

Did you identify what is most important
to the customer?
☐

Did you identify the priorities for you and
your company?
☐

Have you structured your priorities into
SMART goals?
☐

Have you developed success standards for
each SMART goal?
☐

Are you prepared to move to the next
phase of construction?
☐

HACK 7

INSTALL UTILITIES AND MECHANICALS
Develop Your Standard Processes

*It's not the load that breaks you
down, it's the way you carry it.*

— LOU HOLTZ, FOOTBALL COACH

THE PROBLEM: A LACK OF STANDARD PROCESSES LEADS TO FAILURE

IN THE CONSTRUCTION of a home, utilities and mechanicals provide the homeowner with comfort and convenience, confidence in the reliability of those comforts, and a more valuable home. But what if standard processes were not followed in the installation of a home's utilities and mechanicals?

Incorrect installation would lead to system malfunctions, service interruptions, inconveniences, health risks from potential gas and water leaks, increased repair costs, legal issues from building code violations, safety issues from the risk of fire from an electrical short, and possibly complete system failure. What's more, poorly installed and unreliable utilities and mechanicals will decrease the home's resale value, resulting in buyer hesitation to purchase a home with known issues.

A lack of standard processes in your startup can also result in significant problems, such as unclear priorities, poor customer communication, product or service quality issues, insufficient raw materials to make the products, insufficient items in stock to fulfill customer orders, accounting errors leading to non-compliance and legal issues, missed payroll and delivery deadlines, and inattention to safety, leading to employee injuries. It should be clear that a lack of standard processes will lead to a lack of customer confidence in your ability to service them, leading to the potential failure of your new business.

THE HACK: INSTALL UTILITIES AND MECHANICALS

Mapping your day-to-day work involves identifying and executing the daily tasks needed to run your business and serve your customers effectively. For owners, it is also about running the business and not the business running you. Do the work now so you will be prepared when you open for business. For you and your team, this will also create a more effective and productive work environment, lower stress, mitigate the risk of burnout, and increase the chance for long-term success with a quality work-life balance.

Think about mapping your work in the context of proactive versus reactive, and be mindful of two factors:

- *Priorities*: What is most important and brings customer value?

- *Time management*: What is our capacity?

We can apply the basic operational framework with standard processes to any type of business startup. Be prepared to feel inundated with managing, executing, and refining standard processes to deliver the unique value you want to provide for your customers.

Regardless of your type of startup—business-to-business, business-to-consumer, on-site service, manufacturing, distribution, consulting, or mobile business—there are many factors to consider when defining and creating your day-to-day processes to successfully serve your customers and manage your business effectively. Your industry experience or the market analysis you did in Hack 2 will generate thoughts, ideas, and insights on how you want to structure your standard processes for smooth, efficient, and effective day-to-day operations.

To get started with the basic processes you need to develop your operational framework, consider the following questions:

- What day-to-day processes are standard for my business?

- How do I set priorities as an owner?

- What do I do if I do not have the time, workforce, or expertise to perform specific standard processes?

143

Nail It:

The operational and customer service goals you set up in Hack 6 are the roadmap for your day-to-day work priorities.

Operational Framework of Your Standard Processes

The operational framework outlines the business areas where you need to develop your standard processes. Each area describes potential tasks and activities to consider and address.

1. *Sales and Customer Service:* This involves proactive sales activities to prospective customers, following up with current and past customers, and regular communication with customers in the quoting and ordering process to confirm and complete the orders.

2. *Order Processing and Fulfillment:* This involves the entire path of an order, starting from when it is confirmed and continuing through the related work order paperwork; verifying product or service availability; coordinating the assembly, packing, shipping, delivery, and tracking; and invoicing the customer.

3. *Production and Service Delivery:* Production includes the manufacturing of a product or the execution of a service. It involves scheduling sequential tasks and establishing quality standards. There are also service provider (supplier) requirements to coordinate and ensure the timely completion of supplier services.

4. *Inventory and Supplier Management:* Inventory refers to the raw materials used to produce goods and also the finished product you will offer for sale. The task is to manage the quantity of the right items to support the production of those finished products and make them available for customer purchase. Supplier management involves negotiating pricing and payment terms, establishing delivery requirements and schedules, and monitoring the ongoing service reliability and quality of the supplier-provided items you will include in your finished product or service.

5. *Financial Management and Accounting:* Financial management and accounting includes recording all daily monetary transactions, both outbound and inbound (receivables and payables). Many different transactions must be recorded on time. Examples include collecting customer payments from sales, supplier

purchases, other vendor services, and operating expenses like phone services, equipment, and facility leases. Additionally, accounting includes managing cash flow, reconciling business bank accounts, and monitoring accounts receivables and payables to ensure timely invoicing, payments, and collections.

In Hack 11, "Pass the Final Inspection," we will examine software tools and systems that can support and even automate some financial and accounting functions, including payroll administration.

6. *Employee Management and Administration:* This area describes all the tasks and processes to onboard new employees, manage payroll, schedule and track work hours, and administer any benefits you may provide.

7. *Training and Compliance:* Training includes not just the instruction of specific job tasks but also safety training, product training, technical training on office software, soft-skills training on the company values and culture, and diversity training. Compliance includes initiating, maintaining, and updating individual certifications and licenses as required by law, such as a commercial truck or forklift license.

WHAT YOU CAN DO TOMORROW

While many processes will change over time as you learn and grow, establishing the initial regular tasks to organize and run your business is a terrific place to start. Being purposeful in mapping out your initial tasks in each operating area will put your new business in the best position to effectively service customers and make a positive first impression.

- **Identify and list the regular tasks that must be completed.** Use the seven standard process categories listed earlier and write out the regularly required tasks to operate your new business. Develop three lists for the time in which the required task is to be completed: daily, weekly, and monthly.

- **Assign ownership of each regular task.** Assigning ownership for each task in the seven areas of your operational framework will help you determine where the gaps are, whether training will be needed, and whether it makes sense to outsource specific processes such as payroll or bookkeeping.

- **Perform a test sale and list all the steps to complete it.** Create a test sale and walk it through all the steps up to delivery of the product or service to the customer. For example, if you are shipping a product, work with a friend or colleague and ship it to them. If you are starting an in-home cleaning business, clean a friend's house for free and walk through the entire process from the initial client conversation to the final interaction once work is completed. Performing a test sale can help you identify potential steps you may have missed in the process and give you valuable information about the approximate time to complete each step.

- **Make a list of tools and equipment.** The right tools can make the job easier. List tools and equipment that make standard processes easier, safer, and more efficient. These tools and processes may relate to handling materials, packing, and fulfilling orders.

Nail It:

Focus on the tangible benefits of the tool or equipment, and think about the negative impacts if they are absent. The negatives may include not working efficiently, creating safety risks, and compromising a premium customer experience. Tools and equipment are costs but also investments in the value and benefits they provide.

BUILDING MOMENTUM

Mapping your standard processes has two parts. The first is to identify and list all the tasks in each area of the operational framework that must be performed regularly for your startup to function as a formal business, and decide who will be responsible for each regular task. The second is to establish priorities, the timing of when to complete specific tasks, and time estimates of how long the tasks will take to complete.

STEP 1: Prioritize key processes and tasks.

Incorporate your operational and customer service goals and success standards from Hack 6 to establish priorities and drive the delivery of your customer value proposition (CVP).

STEP 2: Establish a regular schedule.

Use your list of the regular tasks that must be completed daily, weekly, and monthly to establish priorities and timing goals in your schedule. You can choose from different scheduling tools, such as a shared calendar you post weekly for your team. I prefer an electronic calendar, such as Google Workspace or Microsoft Outlook, for scheduling and assigning tasks, whether they are repeating or unique one-time tasks to capture, assign, and complete. Find the methods that work best for you and your team.

STEP 3: Plan for contingencies.

In a perfect world, everything would operate smoothly and as planned. However, the world is imperfect. Every business faces adversity and will have to deal with unplanned events. A piece of equipment fails, your phone or computer system goes down, an employee calls in sick, or a customer has a significant problem with the service or product they received. Your priorities and schedule can change quickly. Focus on the priorities that service your customers, look at cross-training members of your team, and plan to have potential backup resources available to fill in when needed.

STEP 4: Set realistic time estimates.

I am all for pushing the limits of what is possible. However, when we push limits, there is a higher risk of failure or poor quality in our work. Be careful to avoid overloading schedules, and allow sufficient time for each task, including a time buffer between task activities.

STEP 5: Start to look for operational efficiencies.

It is never too early to look for operational efficiencies. First, look at the repeatable tasks done many times per day. Finding creative ways to automate or map detailed step-by-step processes fosters accuracy and consistency. A good example is the simple emailed response to customers who fill out a quote request from your website. Rather than retype the email for every individual inquiry, develop a standard response that you have thoughtfully crafted. You can use it as a template and copy it from a document so your customer service team can use it for all emailed responses to customers requesting a quote. You now have speed, consistency, and accuracy in responding to every inquiry, ensuring that every potential customer receives a consistent message about your value proposition.

STEP 6: Establish proactive priorities for yourself.

Getting caught up in the regular schedule of running your day-to-day business is easy. Before you know it, the business is running you. As the owner, including proactive priorities in your schedule is critical. Set aside dedicated time to learn and evaluate your progress in building your business into a well-oiled machine. I recommend that you assess different tasks for refinement and improvement, communicate and collaborate with your team for feedback and coaching, monitor the market to stay current on changes to make potential adjustments, and reach out directly to customers for constructive feedback on their experience in working with your company. We will take a closer look at these proactive activities in Hack 12.

REMOVING OBSTACLES

The challenge in developing standard processes for a new business is that you are always on the clock to get things done efficiently and accurately. You are learning as you go, and in many areas of your business, time management and priorities will become the common obstacles. Here are questions about common trip-ups, and my responses.

What if we do not have time to get everything done? As an owner and business leader, I would hear this statement from a member of my team, and it sounded like this in my mind: *"It was not a priority."* As the owner, you are constantly learning and refining the time it takes to complete different standard processes. Use communication and collaboration with your team to reinforce priorities and problem-solve what adjustments to make to complete tasks in the time needed to service your customers.

What if some employees take longer than others to complete the same tasks? We all have different strengths and weaknesses, and you will have members of your team who perform better and faster at certain tasks than others. A good strategy to address this challenge is to lean on the person who performs the specific task the best. Enlist this person to share and train others on the refined process to set a standard benchmark to improve further. I recommend being a strengths-based leader. Share that you are a team, learning together, and each of you (including you as the owner) has strengths and weaknesses. Your collective goal is to learn and improve together every day, and you can support this when you match each individual's strengths with the assigned roles and tasks that are best suited for them.

What if I don't have the time and expertise to do it all as a one-person business owner? Where do you bring the most value as the owner in growing and running your business? If you are a one-employee business, look strategically at your standard processes and explore outside resources for support. Many cost-effective outside resources are available for small businesses today. You must sell your services and fulfill the orders. Think about the best use of your focused time.

THE HACK IN ACTION

Nancy was the owner of White Glove Cleaners. She had retired from her teaching career and was preparing to launch her new business. She worked for five years for a home cleaning company during the summers while teaching full time. She had dreamed of running her own business and building a team of home cleaning experts. Her website was ready to go with a list of the different cleaning services she would offer, a quote request form that collected customer information, and other details, such as the square footage of the home, the number of bedrooms, and the standard and specialty service options.

She had a few clients already lined up and was confident in the cleaning process from her experience as an employee cleaning homes. Still, being a new business owner, she needed to map out all the other day-to-day processes to operate as a functional business. Nancy hired a couple of team members to perform the in-home cleaning services, and she planned to add additional cleaning employees as the company grew.

Here's how Nancy planned her standard processes according to the six steps in the prior Building Momentum section.

STEP 1: Prioritize key processes and tasks.

She made a list of the regular tasks to complete in each of the seven areas of her operational framework, their frequency, and who would perform each task. Nancy was concerned that she would not have the expertise to complete specific standard processes, and she believed her time would be better spent focused on the clients. She decided to look to outside resources for payroll administration, financial management, and accounting processes. Her accountant recommended a payroll service that could handle weekly payroll and all the steps and forms to onboard new employees. Nancy was not an accountant, so she hired an accounting firm to handle bookkeeping and compile monthly financial statements. See Table 7.1 for Nancy's list of standard process tasks. (Download a blank template version to use for your business at ronneary.com.)

Standard Process Tasks	Frequency	Who
1. Sales and Customer Service		
Sales and quoting	Daily	Nancy
2. Order Processing and Fulfillment		
Invoicing and collecting payment	Daily	Nancy
3. Production and Service Delivery		
Coordinating customer cleaning schedules	Daily	Nancy
Performing home cleaning services	Daily	Cleaning Crew
4. Inventory and Supplier Management		
Managing cleaning supplies	Weekly	Nancy
5. Financial Management and Accounting		
Logging payable and receivable transactions	Daily	Bookkeeper
Reconciling business bank accounts	Weekly	Bookkeeper
Completing financial statements	Monthly	Accountant
Paying taxes	Monthly	Accountant
6. Employee Management and Administration		
Scheduling and tracking work hours	Weekly	Nancy
Employee onboarding and payroll	Weekly	Payroll Partner
7. Training and Compliance		
Training and coordinating the cleaning process	Weekly	Nancy

Table 7.1

STEP 2: Establish a regular schedule.

After listing all the regular tasks, Nancy decided to establish a daily schedule to manage her time and priority deadlines for each task effectively. From her teaching days, she was an expert user of Google Calendar and decided it would be her tool for staying on schedule and managing cleaning schedules with her employees.

STEP 3: Plan for contingencies.

Thinking through the weekly customer cleaning schedules, Nancy thought she should have a backup in case one of her two cleaners was unavailable. She decided that to keep her customers happy and not disrupt their weekly cleaning service, she would be the backup person. She also found someone who could be available part-time and "on call" if needed to fill in.

STEP 4: Set realistic time estimates.

Nancy realized she would need to account for travel time between customer homes in the cleaning schedules. With the time it would take to clean a home based on the client's requested services, knowing that sometimes it might take longer to clean specific clients' houses, she planned an hour between the departure from one house and the arrival at the next.

STEP 5: Start to look for operational efficiencies.

As part of her process to look for efficiencies, Nancy performed a test run of her business services. She offered a 50 percent discount to two of her new clients if they would walk through the process with her and provide feedback on the experience. Overall, the cleaning went well, but she learned there were a couple of miscommunications in scheduling and understanding the cleaning tasks to complete. Also, her invoicing email ended up in the client's spam folder, and the pay-by-credit-card option needed more precise instructions for the client. All were easy fixes, and she learned that the miscommunication was due to her employee calling the client to confirm the time they would arrive. With no caller ID, the client ignored the call. Nancy realized she had to update her quote form to include asking the client for their preferred method of communication.

As for other efficiencies, Nancy was specific about the cleaning process and the supplies they would use. She needed to ensure her cleaners would have the cleaning supplies readily available. In the test run, the cleaners had to stop at her house to pick up the supplies. She quickly learned that shipping the cleaning supplies directly to her cleaners would save time so they would not have to stop at her house to pick them up.

STEP 6: Establish proactive priorities for yourself.

Before Nancy got too caught up in the day-to-day tasks of running the business, she wanted to include a couple of priorities in her schedule. She wanted to commit time to reaching out to clients directly for regular feedback. She also decided to schedule a weekly check-in meeting with her team to share client feedback and discuss areas where they could improve their services, share best practices, communicate more effectively, and become more efficient.

Nancy knew that as the business grew, she would need to adjust schedules, priorities, and time management. By mapping out the regular tasks and processes and performing a couple of test runs with clients, she felt confident that she had established a solid operational framework for launching her cleaning service.

The goal of mapping day-to-day work is to identify the regular tasks you must do to run your business effectively, bring order to chaos, and build on what you will learn every day to continuously improve the customer experience while maximizing profitability. Here's a summary of the guidance in this Hack:

Test and learn. With online reviews of the customer experience given early and often and readily available for other potential customers, you only get one chance to make a first impression. If you need to perform more than one test sale to refine the customer experience, by all means, test and learn until you get it right, and then build a continuous improvement culture.

Document workflows. Mapping is a method that promotes a better understanding of your processes. Document your workflows so you have a clearly defined starting point for you and your team. I am a whiteboard junkie who thrives on capturing processes visually and collaborating with the team on troubleshooting and improving. I recommend this process to you because it works.

Commit to your proactive priorities. I worked for an owner early in my career, and I was amazed at how in tune he was with the regular operation of the business and, at the same time, how knowledgeable, forward-thinking, focused, and strategic about where the company was going and what we needed to do next. I asked him how he was able to stay on top of so many day-to-day activities and, at the same time, drive the business forward. His reply was simple: "I do not deviate from the proactive priorities I set for myself. They are just as important as the day-to-day items if we are going to continue to improve and succeed." I learned that he had a high level of discipline in setting time limits when focusing on different areas of the business. Once he reached the time limit for working on a specific area, he moved on to the next proactive priority item on his list.

As an owner, you will face many demands on your time from many directions, and you'll need to find a balance between your reactive and proactive priorities so you can run your business and not let it run you.

Use the following checklist to help you stay organized with your progress.

HACK 7
INSTALL UTILITIES AND MECHANICALS

Completed

Have you listed *all* the regular tasks that you must complete? ☐

Have you arranged to run one or more test sales? ☐

Have you established a *daily, weekly,* and *monthly* schedule? ☐

Did you establish proactive priorities for yourself? ☐

Are you prepared to move to the next phase of construction? ☐

HACK 8

BUILD THE ROOFING SYSTEM
Implement Your Marketing Strategies

Master the topic, the message, and the delivery.
— STEVE JOBS, FOUNDER AND CEO OF APPLE

THE PROBLEM: INEFFECTIVE MARKETING MEANS MISSED OPPORTUNITIES

A HOME'S ROOF IS critical to protecting the investment of everything under it. A roofing system comprises many components that must be installed properly and work together to be effective.

So, what if the roofer missed installing some components and installed others improperly? Your new home would experience problems such as water leaks and damage to the interior, including ceilings, walls, insulation, floors, and essentially everything under the roof that the system was intended to protect. More significant problems could include health risks from the growth of mold and mildew or a collapsed roof, compromising the structural integrity of the home.

The lack of effective marketing strategies can also lead to significant problems, including a limited reach to your ideal target audience, a misunderstanding of your customer value proposition, poor brand awareness, missed opportunities, and stagnant sales.

Most startups have limited budgets. As a result, marketing resources must be used efficiently to gain new customers and effectively grow the business. Competitors with better marketing strategies can capture a larger market share, putting your business at a disadvantage. Not implementing effective marketing strategies or gathering a basic understanding of how effective marketing works can lead to dismal sales and profit shortfalls, ultimately causing the business to fail.

THE HACK: BUILD THE ROOFING SYSTEM

You must get the word out about your startup and share that you are open for business and ready to serve. Since nothing happens until you make a sale, you will have to understand who you want to sell to, how to reach them, how you will interact with them, and how you will earn their business.

To reach customers, you need to develop and implement effective marketing strategies. The purpose of marketing is to connect with, engage, and motivate potential customers to learn more about your business and purchase your products and services.

Key questions to consider:

- Who is your ideal target audience?
- How will customers find you and learn about your company, products, and services?
- What perception do you want customers to have of your business?
- What digital presence should your business have?
- What proactive marketing strategies should you use to reach target customers?

In today's digital world, most startup businesses can engage in effective and affordable marketing strategies, such as a social media presence, e-marketing, and social media campaigns—all anchored by a simple website. The beauty of digital marketing is that your product or service can reach virtually anywhere almost instantaneously. The drawback, however, is that your brand-new business risks getting lost in the crowd if you are not careful and deliberate in your marketing strategy.

WHAT YOU CAN DO TOMORROW

- **Zero in on your target audience.** Start by developing a profile of your ideal customers, their needs and preferences, and the problems your solution solves. This will provide focus and guidance for your marketing efforts. Revisit what you learned in your detailed market analysis to further understand your target audience.

- **Audit marketing strategies of competitors.** In Hack 2, "Lay a Solid Foundation," you did a detailed market analysis and identified key direct competitors and other similar businesses in non-competitive markets where you will not compete directly. Take a closer look at the marketing elements of their businesses, such as:

  ▸ **Social media presence** – What social media platforms are they using? Facebook, X (Twitter), Instagram, LinkedIn, or YouTube?

  ▸ **Website** – Do they have a website? What is your initial impression as a visitor? When auditing a website, look for key elements such as content, design, site structure, and ease of navigation.

> ▸ *Content.* Compare keywords and phrases to your list. How do they present their customer value and unique selling proposition? Do they share pricing for their product or service?

> ▸ *Design and structure.* Does the website have a premium feel with quality photos and graphics? How many pages does the site have, and what are the page titles?

> ▸ *Calls to action.* Is there a contact form, quote request form, link to join the mailing list, promotional offer, or live chat?

▸ **Brand presentation** – Does their brand project a confident, professional look and feel? Does their logo project professionalism?

▸ **Promotions and discounts** – Are they actively pursuing customers with promotions, discounts, referrals, or memberships to follow them for updates about new products, services, or offers?

▸ **Customer reviews** - Conduct a Google search for customer reviews of their business. What are customer impressions of their products or services, and what do customers say about the experience of working with them?

BUILDING MOMENTUM

Marketing strategies raise awareness of your business, establish your brand identity, communicate who you are, share the products and services you offer, provide a call to action, and allow potential customers to connect with you. Developing basic marketing strategies early on will help alleviate the stress of reaching your ideal customer amid the exciting buildup of other aspects of your new venture.

STEP 1: Start building your brand identity.

You have developed your CVP and zeroed in on your ideal target audience. Your brand identity is the consistent messaging representing your business, values, and what your business offers in service to customers. Your brand identity is represented in words and visuals, including a memorable logo and color scheme, to motivate customers to choose you over your competitors.

The company logo is the symbol you will use consistently throughout all your marketing initiatives. You can find many options to generate a company logo: free online tools, paid online graphic design firms, a talented friend, a freelance graphic designer, or local brand design firms.

Be mindful of the different mediums in which your logo will be used, such as digitally on a website or on social media and printed on business cards, letterhead, customer estimates, proposals, banners, and even vehicles or clothing. Enlist feedback from friends, colleagues, and test customers. Remember, like many other elements of your new business, the logo can be refined as you learn and grow.

STEP 2: Establish a social media presence.

Social media platforms offer a simple and low-cost (most are free) means to establish a digital presence for your startup. Choose the platforms where your target audience is most active and create a profile on those platforms for your new business. To engage with your potential target customers, focus on posting content that would be interesting and bring value. Lastly, make sure you consistently represent your brand identity and contact information.

Here is a list of popular social media platforms with the aspects of each that can add to your social media outreach:

- **Facebook** – It's still relevant. This platform has a large user base, meaning a larger demographic reach. In addition, pages and groups on this platform build brand visibility.

- **Instagram** – It's trendy. You can engage your audience through videos, images, and stories. This platform is known for visual storytelling to build your brand identity.

- **LinkedIn** – It's the leading professional networking platform. LinkedIn will allow you targeted advertising options for B2B businesses. You can also combine personal profiles and company profiles for maximum impact.

- **YouTube** – This is the dominant platform for video content. There's rapid brand growth here through tutorials, demos, and video blogs. You can increase engagement through comments and subscriptions to your channel.

STEP 3: Learn to use email marketing.

Email marketing is another low-cost and relatively easy-to-execute marketing strategy that involves proactively sending emails to customers who are engaged with your business. Email marketing became popular in the mid-1990s and is still an effective digital marketing tool today. However, the biggest downside to e-marketing is that businesses can inundate consumers with too many messages.

Create a schedule of when to send emails. Once a week or every other week is good practice. You want to stay relevant and also respect your customers' time.

Content should offer more than just promoting your company; ideally, it provides relevant and valuable current information about your industry, market, or business segment. You can also include information about new products or services, promotions, and discounts with a call to action for customers to contact you for more information.

Here is a list of popular e-marketing platforms for small businesses:

- **Mailchimp** – This is an easy-to-use, AI-available content creator offering a variety of design templates to choose from and responsive customer support.

- **Constant Contact** – This is also an easy-to-use, AI-available content creator. It has a user-friendly interface but limited customization options, and it can be expensive as an email list grows.

- **MailBluster** – This is a cost-effective option. It's intuitive and user-friendly, and there's no limit on the number of email campaigns you can send.

- **Moosend** – This is another easy-to-use, AI-available content creator. The design templates are easily customizable, and the app offers customer support.

STEP 4: Identify networking opportunities.

In Hack 2, you researched industry associations, potential trade shows and conferences, and trade groups. Put what you learned to work: identify networking opportunities through local chapters of trade groups, sign up to display at a trade show, become active in a trade group, or attend a conference.

If you are a local business serving the local community, you can participate in community events such as fairs, festivals, or farmers' markets, or you can volunteer in a local charity to build goodwill and connect directly with others in the community to network your business. You may host an event, such as an open house or workshop, to showcase your new business and industry expertise and network with potential new customers.

You can also network with other businesses that complement your business to cross-promote each other and encourage mutual referrals. For example, if your business is window cleaning, you may want to network and cross-promote with a home builder or window replacement company, offering them a small financial perk and a discount to the client when you sell to a new client they referred.

STEP 5: Implement promotion, incentive, and referral strategies.

A highly effective strategy to gain new customers is to incentivize existing customers to refer others to your business by word-of-mouth recommendations. A referral program is cost-effective, easy to set up, and a valuable marketing tool for a startup to build a customer base quickly. Choose an incentive that aligns with your business goals, such as a discount on a future purchase, cash incentive, or free product or service.

Promotions and incentives can be effective marketing strategies for creating urgency and motivating potential customers to try your product or service. Examples include coupons, limited-time offers, and one-time discounts for high-profile customers who agree to provide a written positive review and recommendation.

REMOVING OBSTACLES

Obstacles to marketing your startup can come in many forms, including a lack of technical expertise in digital marketing, doubt about whether you are putting your effort and energy into the right marketing strategies, or questions about the ideal use of social media platforms. You may also get frustrated when trying to come up with new topics and keep social media content fresh and interesting to build your brand identity without sounding like you are asking for business with every post. Here are solutions to those obstacles.

How long should it take to build my brand identity? Building your brand identity never stops. Every marketing strategy you initiate and every customer interaction is an opportunity to build, reinforce, and enhance your brand identity. The key is to be consistent in your messaging about who you are and the value you commit to delivering to current *and* new customers.

How do I know if I am using the right social media platforms? Zeroing in on your target audience will help you choose the best social media platform to promote your business. For example, if your target audience is older, you may want to be on Facebook. Conversely, if your target audience is single young people, Instagram is a better option. Considering that there is little or no cost for a social media presence, and the platforms are constantly evolving, participating on multiple platforms is a good practice.

Do I have to become a marketing expert? Yes and no. As an entrepreneur, you are the expert on the products, services, and value you provide for potential customers. You may decide to work with an outside marketing resource for their experience and creative expertise, but *you* are the content and messaging expert for your business.

What if I am not tech-savvy enough to effectively use digital tools? It can be stressful if you are not tech-savvy. Consider the best use of your time and the importance of successfully using digital marketing tools. Save yourself from the stress and frustration and find someone who is tech-savvy. They are plentiful. You could enlist the help of a friend or family member. Young people grew up with technology, and finding someone more well-versed in social media platforms to help you should be easy and affordable. Hiring a freelance tech expert is also a reasonable option.

Do I need a website? I highly recommend that you build a website for your business. It is the "digital anchor" of all your marketing efforts. However, not every startup needs a website to launch its new business. A good social media presence—where you can engage with customers and share the basics, such as who you are, what products and services you offer, and the value you provide—can also be effective as you get started.

Nail It:

If you create a website for your startup, I highly recommend including FAQs. Potential customers visiting your website have questions and are looking for answers. They will quickly navigate to your FAQs to find the answer they seek. You can develop the initial list of FAQs from the questions customers or potential customers ask you.

THE HACK IN ACTION

Mary and Madison were college juniors and education majors. They excelled academically in high school and became friends, both tutoring younger classmates during their senior year. Together, they decided to put their tutoring experience, passion for teaching, and ongoing college education to work by starting a tutoring business.

Mary and Madison needed to develop their marketing strategies to get the word out that M&M Tutoring was open for business. To build credibility (brand identity) for their new business, they sent out a message that they were alumni from the high school, education majors at the local university, and part of the school community. They even created their brand logo in the high school colors.

They decided it made the most sense to focus their efforts on freshmen and sophomore students and parents from their old high school. They knew the school and staff well, making networking with teachers and parents easy. They were both savvy social media users and researched tutoring services for insight into how other tutoring service providers presented their services, messaging, pricing, and other details. They decided the best way to target students, parents, and teachers was to utilize Instagram, Facebook, and LinkedIn. They found many social media groups they could join to connect, engage, and promote M&M Tutoring.

Responses were slow initially, so Mary and Madison put together a 25 percent discount coupon for the first session and a 25 percent discount for referrals. To get the word out on the discount promotion, they posted details on their social media platforms and attended various school events and sports games for in-person promotions. They also connected with a couple of their favorite teachers from the high school and gained testimonial endorsements, adding more credibility and exposure to their new venture.

To keep their promos fresh and drive regular engagement, they devised an informational social media campaign. They posted a weekly FAQ on the benefits of tutoring during the freshman and sophomore years and asked parents and students to submit their questions. Mary and Madison also planned a website and future email marketing. Soon after launching M&M Tutoring, the business began to grow and has been successful through its simple and effective marketing strategies and social media following.

Not everyone is a marketing expert. Tools and strategies to effectively market products and services evolve and change over time. Customers' wants and needs change over time. As the owner, *you* will need to learn, grow, and change to become the marketing content expert for your business. In the startup stage, you are putting together your initial marketing strategies to invite customers to learn more about your business. It is critical to present your business professionally, your products and services effectively, and your unique customer value proposition flawlessly.

The most effective and successful small-business owners have an incredible appetite for continuously learning from and engaging with customers. Over the years, I have told many of my marketing and sales teams that it is what you ask and learn, not what you say and know, that makes the difference.

Use the following checklist to help you stay organized with your progress.

HACK 8
BUILD THE ROOFING SYSTEM

Completed

Have you zeroed in on your target audience? ☐

Have you laid out your brand identity? ☐

Did you decide on social media platforms that align with your target audience? ☐

Did you identify at least four to six networking opportunities? ☐

Are you prepared to move to the next phase of construction? ☐

HACK 9

ADD EXTERIOR ELEMENTS
Choose Your Sales Approach

*You only get one chance to
make a first impression.*

— OFTEN ATTRIBUTED TO OSCAR WILDE, POET AND PLAYWRIGHT

THE PROBLEM: PASSION FOR YOUR BUSINESS DOES NOT EQUAL EFFECTIVE SALES TECHNIQUES

IN THE CONSTRUCTION industry, the exterior elements provide curb appeal and are the first impression of a home. Exterior elements are driven by both design and performance. From a design perspective, the siding, trim, colors, architectural accents (stone, hardware, shutters), and windows and doors can inspire the buyer to want to learn more and see what is inside the home.

All these elements must be properly installed and in the right sequence for fit and finish to protect the home from the elements. What if your custom home builder did not carefully learn and understand what you wanted in the design and performance of the exterior elements and made assumptions about what you would like? The result would not be positive. The wrong colors, wrong materials, and poor quality would only increase your disgust with your builder's lack of interest in understanding your needs and preferences.

Not choosing the right sales approach can also leave a poor first impression on potential customers. If you do not ask the right questions to learn and understand their needs, you will not know if your product or service is the right solution, and nor will they.

The result is a customer who will respond with a "No" to your company when making their buying decision. This lack of understanding of the buyer's needs can lead to frustration over why they chose not to do business with you.

This leads to wasted time and effort, a lack of trust and confidence from the potential customer, misdirected marketing efforts, limited repeat business, poor referrals, and missed opportunities for candid customer feedback for the product or service improvement. It can also lead you to question whether you have the right customer value proposition. A business must make sales to survive, so the lack of new customers and sales will put the company at risk of financial failure.

THE HACK: ADD EXTERIOR ELEMENTS

When choosing your sales approach, consider these key questions:

- Do you understand the customer's decision-making process?

- How do you identify prospective customers?
- How will you determine whether your solution will meet their needs?
- What sales support tools will you need?
- Are you comfortable asking for the sale?
- How will you gain customer referrals?

If your product or service is directed at other businesses and requires a longer, more formal sales approach, it is a good practice to develop your sales strategy into a systematic process. If your business requires you to contact prospective customers directly and engage them in conversation, following a repeatable and step-by-step process makes sense.

I am a common sense, pragmatic, solution-oriented salesperson, sales leader, and sales trainer. Having been in several sales roles during my career, I stumbled with my effectiveness in several of them. Eighteen years ago, I was introduced to a sales methodology that naturally follows the buyer's decision-making process. It was not high-pressure and taught me to ask the right questions, listen, learn, and confirm I clearly understood the customer's needs. My "aha moment" was when I realized that sales is a business discipline, just like purchasing or accounting, with its own methods, processes, theories, and ways to learn.

Even if your product or service is in retail or e-commerce, where customers make buying decisions with minimal direct interaction, it is still important to approach sales as a discipline. Understanding the customer's decision-making process is crucial, and engaging with customers for direct feedback is essential for learning and continuous improvement.

WHAT YOU CAN DO TOMORROW

I'm pleased to share the basic framework of the sales methodology I have used for many years, taught, and recommended to others when selling business-to-business. It is called Action Selling Professional Sales Training Programs. The processes are based on common sense and easy to follow by those who sincerely want to develop trust in a customer relationship, communicate effectively, and determine whether their solution can bring value in service to a customer.

- **Understand the five buyer decisions.** We are all customers and make buying decisions when we want to make a purchase. The five steps shown in Table 9.1 are typically made in sequence, and once we decide "yes" on each buying decision, we move on to the next. Answering "yes" to each one completes the purchase transaction.

A Buyer's Decision-Making Process

Buying Decision	Buyer Questions
Salesperson	Do I feel I can trust this person? Do I think I can work with them?
Company	Do I have confidence the company can deliver what I need? Is this a company I would feel comfortable working with?
Solution	Is it the right solution to meet my needs? Does the solution bring me value?
Price	Is the solution at the right price? Does the solution help me make money or save money?
Time to buy	When is the right time to complete the transaction?

Table 9.1

- **Develop target customer profile criteria.** In Hack 8, you zeroed in on your ideal target audience. Detailed customer profiles will help you prioritize the target customers you want to contact first to begin the sales process. See Table 9.2 for example criteria, and download a template for your business at ronneary.com.

Customer profile criteria examples

Industry and Markets	Are they in the industry and markets you want to be in?
Company Size	Does their revenue provide insight into the potential size of the opportunity for your business?
Location	Do they do business in the geographic markets that you want to be in?
Market Position	What is the age of the company? Are they market leaders? Are they growing or trending upward?
Key Roles	Can you identify the people and decision-makers you need to connect with to start the sales process?
News and Current Events	What is new with their company? What recent events, happenings, and milestones are trending?

Table 9.2

- **Identify and make a list of target customers.** Use the research skills learned in Hack 2 and scope out the market to make a list of specific target customers you would like to sell to. Use your customer profile criteria as you conduct your research to qualify opportunities and prioritize your target list.

BUILDING MOMENTUM

Now that you're giving more thought to your "exterior elements"—the sales approach to reach your target audience—you're ready to follow a step-by-step process to make the sales and close the deals.

STEP 1: Refine and polish your people skills.

Not all of us have experience in the role of a salesperson. Many people are not comfortable in that role. Brushing up on your people skills is the first step because you only get one chance to make a first impression, and the first buying decision is about *you*. Presenting yourself as the owner and decision-maker for your business does bring initial credibility. The customer's "yes" decision lies in your ability to facilitate effective, professional communication while building confidence and trust.

Refining your people skills includes three tasks:

- *Brief introduction about yourself*: State who you are and your role and responsibilities at your new company. Share a few sentences about your relevant experience to establish credibility.

- *Build rapport and show your interest*: A positive attitude is key. Smile, be friendly, and remember people's names. Show genuine interest in learning about them and their business.

- *Be a good listener*: Too often, we wait to talk instead of actively listening during verbal communication. Now is the time to prioritize active listening. One strategy is to prepare a list of questions to help you stay focused on listening and learning.

STEP 2: Prepare a list of open-ended questions.

You can only determine whether your solution meets the customer's needs by asking questions and actively listening and learning. Prepare a short list of open-ended questions to ask prospective customers about what matters most to them when considering purchasing the type of product or service you offer.

Examples of open-ended questions:

- Can you share a little about yourself and how you got to the role you're in?

- How does your company differentiate itself from your competitors?

- What do you look for in an ideal supplier for product-X or service-X?

- What are the opportunities for improvement with your current product or service?

- What other factors are necessary for you when considering a different supplier?

Nail It:

Take notes. Writing down what someone says is a compliment to the speaker, demonstrating your full attention and desire to capture key points. If you're worried this might seem rude to the customer, simply explain that you want to capture their thoughts and perspectives accurately.

STEP 3: Develop your company story.

Compile a brief statement you can confidently deliver about your company's identity, what it does, and how it is different from your competition. It should also describe your value of service in the customer relationship.

Here's a good example of a company story by a graphic design business: "My business partner and I started our graphic design business earlier this year. We have over thirty-four years combined of experience in creative design, including visual identity design, print design, web design, and package design. Our mission is to work collaboratively with clients throughout the creative process to exceed client design expectations and provide the work on time and within budget."

STEP 4: Determine sales support tools.

Sales support tools highlight your product or service to prospective customers. Their primary purpose is to assist you in detailing and demonstrating your offerings, ultimately helping you close the sale. Sales support tools may include brochures, samples, case studies, technical documents, and installation instructions.

- *The power of paper*: If you are selling a product, would it benefit the customer to see it, touch it, feel it, and demonstrate its performance characteristics for them to make the purchase decision? In this digital age, there is still value in printed sales support materials. Small businesses can format such documents to standard paper sizes and print them in-house to save money. Any printed sales support tools can also be made available digitally (most commonly in PDF format) and conveniently shared electronically with prospective customers.

- *Everyone loves samples*: If you decide you need to have product samples to support the sales process, think through their presentation so they include branding and labeling with features, benefits, and specifications. Even the packaging should be well-designed and represent your brand, including your website address and contact information. Product samples can be costly, so to create the best, most effective samples, develop different prototype options, test them and learn with your team, and share them with your test sales candidates for constructive feedback.

- *A little story goes a long way*: Company brochures, like samples, should look professional. Carefully choose the size, layout, branding, website, contact information, high-quality photography, and print material. Digital printing is a significant advantage today, allowing for much smaller quantities to be produced at one time to help minimize costs. Hiring a professional graphic designer to help you through the process and technical layout elements is well worth the investment.

STEP 5: Present your product or service.

Presenting your product or service reflects your work to learn about their business and how your solution can meet customers' needs. You will demonstrate and review sam ples of your product and its features and benefits or review your services in detail to provide clarity to the customer. Presenting your product or service should directly demonstrate how you can effectively meet or exceed their needs.

STEP 6: Ask for the business.

It appears straightforward, but it's not easy for everyone to do. According to information published by Action Selling in 2024, 63 percent of salespeople directly ask the customer to commit to the purchase, which means 37 percent do not ask. There are many reasons why salespeople may be reluctant to ask for the business, such as fear of rejection, lack of confidence, worries about being too pushy, or overthinking it. Know that if you are going to be successful, you must be able to directly ask for the business. Summarize the benefits that meet each potential customer's needs, quote the price, and ask for the business.

Phrasing options to ask for the sale:

- Would you like to go ahead with this?
- Will this work for you?
- Would you like to move forward?
- Are you ready to move forward with the purchase?

Nail It:

Once you ask for the business, stop talking and wait patiently for an answer. If you have asked the right questions, confirmed the customer's needs, presented how your solution meets or exceeds those needs, and quoted a price—then ask for the business and wait for a response.

STEP 7: Set goals and track your progress.

In Hack 6, we covered goal-setting and success standards. The same fundamentals apply to sales. Goal-setting drives behaviors and priorities. Rejection can be discouraging, so keep yourself and your salespeople focused on tasks, set goals, and track your progress.

Be SMART and realistic in developing your sales goals. They should follow the SMART goal-setting format and be attainable based on relentless efforts and your capacity to deliver. Some sales goals are measured in ways other than sales dollars and are often broken down into individual salesperson-assigned goals.

Specific sales goal examples include:

- Gain ten new customers by the end of the first quarter.

- Sell ten new add-on services to the standard contract by the end of the second quarter.

- Get two referrals from each new customer gained each month.

- Sell five new contracts in the south suburb in the first half of the year.

- Identify twenty new sales target prospects for standard service contracts in a defined market area by the end of the month.

Progress is commonly tracked by reports of monthly sales dollars broken down by specific preferences and compared against goals. Specific sales goals are often straightforward and easier to track for startups with a smaller initial focus.

REMOVING OBSTACLES

Here are common questions about areas where business owners struggle with their sales and marketing efforts, followed by experience-based guidance.

What if a target customer does not contact us after our marketing efforts? In sales, the action often taken when a target customer does not respond to your initial marketing efforts is called a "cold call." A cold call is reaching out to customers directly when they have no idea who you are and no knowledge of your business or the value you can provide through your products or services. Cold calling is stressful and difficult for many, and rejection is common.

I recommend making what I refer to as a "warm call" to begin connecting directly and engaging with a target customer. The goal of the warm call is to establish a relationship and convey that you care about helping them solve their problems or improve their business. Here are some tips to help you get started warm-calling potential customers.

- Prepare
  - ► Identify the contact and their role with the company.

- ► Research the current state of the company and its products and services.

- Message electronically
  - ► Send an email or social media message to set the context.
  - ► Show your knowledge of the industry and what you have learned about their company, and share who you are and your company story message.
  - ► State your motivation to learn more about their business and whether you could find mutual value in working together.
  - ► Ask for an appointment at a convenient time to connect directly.

- Follow up
  - ► Chances are, they may not respond to your message.
  - ► You have warmed them up with your electronic message and provided clear context about your purpose in reaching out.
  - ► Call them directly; now you are simply following up on your message.
  - ► Restate your purpose and ask for an appointment at a convenient time.

What if I am just not comfortable as a salesperson? If you are uncomfortable selling, you will need to get comfortable quickly, as sales fuel your business engine. Starting a new business means getting outside your comfort zone and pushing yourself. As the owner and decision-maker, *you must engage with customers* to learn, adjust, and continuously improve to succeed.

How can I improve my people skills? Some of us are introverts and struggle with being outgoing, meeting new people, building rapport, and proactively establishing new relationships. You can take three practical steps to refine and polish your people skills:

- *Create a script*: Capture your messaging in writing. Soon, you will commit it to memory, and your delivery will become natural, smooth, and concise.

- *Be consistent*: Follow the sales process consistently. Prepare your questions and write down the steps to keep you focused on the sequential buying decisions.

- *Learn by doing*: Stay positive! You will improve through repetition, and engaging with customers will become more comfortable and effective.

How can I be sure that our solution meets the customer's needs? The customer's agreement will confirm whether your solution meets their needs. It's really that simple. If you are not sure, *ask.* You asked good open-ended questions to get them to open up about what is important to them and what they need. Review your notes from your questions and revisit the conversation. Ask them, "Does our product or service meet your needs?"

What if I am not sure who makes the final purchase decision? Clarifying the decision-maker can be tricky. Some may influence the decision, and some may qualify your product or service. It may come down to one decision-maker or a group decision. To clarify, ask who is involved in the decision-making process, their roles, and who makes the final buying decision.

How will I know if the customer is considering other suppliers? Building rapport with the customer is valuable because it leads to an open discussion. It is in your best interest to ask if the customer is considering other suppliers in order to position how your solution is different and better. You can ask this open-ended question to clarify: "What other potential vendors or suppliers are you considering in your decision-making process?"

THE HACK IN ACTION

Kevin is a creative and talented graphic designer. He worked as a graphic designer in the marketing department of a product manufacturing company for eleven years, but when his work felt repetitive and less creative, he did some creative side work. Then, he left his full-time marketing department job.

He is talented in turning a client's vision into a graphic representation. The director of marketing assigned him clients at his old job, and his side work was based on referrals from coworkers and others in his professional circles.

Kevin's biggest concern about working independently was selling his talents and services to new clients with whom he did not already have a rapport or relationship. He was also unsure about what types of prospective customers would make the most sense for him to reach out to.

As Kevin began to build his business based on his work experience at the product manufacturing company, he decided his graphic services would be the most valuable to similar companies, so he zeroed in on his target audience and put together profile criteria comparable to his work history to develop his target list. He realized he could conduct virtual meetings that would remove any limits on working with only local companies. He created a prioritized target list of thirty companies that fit his customer profile criteria, and he implemented his marketing strategies to the companies on the list and his professional network connections to get the word out about his new graphic design business.

He learned from the five buying decisions (earlier in this Hack) that he served as three of the five buying decisions for potential clients: the salesperson, the company, and his work as the solution. He scripted his company story that covered the first three buying decisions (salesperson, company, solutions) to make a consistent and positive first impression in his initial conversation with target customers. He came up with the following "Solutions Story" script to help him reach his target customers:

> *I have worked as a creative graphic designer for the past ten years, specializing in company brand development and product branding, including brochures, technical documents, and packaging design. Working in the marketing department of a larger company gave me the opportunity to use the best graphic program technologies, which I also use in my business. My company mission is to collaborate with clients to translate their stated vision into the most effective graphic representations to support their business's value messaging, growth, and success.*

Kevin put together a list of open-ended questions that he believed would help him get the client to open up and share what they wanted and needed in graphic services. For example, he asked, "What are the goals for your marketing department?" and "Can you share a little about what an ideal graphic design resource could do for you?"

He developed three sales support tools to enhance his presentation of work and services. The first was a portfolio featuring examples of his work that he could share in print or send electronically to potential customers. The second was a brochure that communicated his company's mission and services. The third tool was a proposal template to outline the scope of work and the client process, including project milestones and pricing.

Nail It:

Add a QR code in your brochure or other marketing materials to allow clients to scan it with their smartphones to review an electronic version of your company or portfolio of work.

Kevin received a few target customer inquiries from his marketing strategies. It was a good start, but he knew he needed to reach out directly if he was going to build his client base. Kevin did not consider himself a salesperson and was nervous about initiating contact. He used the "warm call" method to identify key contacts and learn as much as possible about their business and marketing teams. He messaged the key contacts through LinkedIn, sharing what he had learned about their companies and that he was eager to learn more, asking if there was a good time to connect directly for a short conversation. Kevin followed up with each of them and connected directly with nine of the remaining twenty-seven on his target list. He used his prepared open-ended questions to identify opportunities to gain graphic design work.

He set a goal to gain six new clients from his target list of thirty, thinking that is what he could handle as a one-person graphic design firm. He gained five new clients from his sales efforts. Additionally, Kevin learned that having a consistent sales approach with his company story, prepared open-ended questions, simple sales support tools, and the "warm call" method made him feel more comfortable selling his graphic design services. With repetition from a consistent approach, he also became more effective, and it felt more natural to ask potential new customers for a commitment to work with him.

Nothing happens in a business until a sale is made. There are no orders to process, nothing to pack up and ship, no invoices to send, no money to collect, and no profit. Too often, startup businesses overlook the importance of having a consistent, repeatable, systematic sales approach. To become effective at selling, you need to develop your craft through practice, repetition, learning, and continuous improvement.

Selling, in its simplest description, is problem-solving. Clearly understand the problem and determine whether your business offers a good solution. Over the years, when my teams followed our systematic sales approach and learned that we were not a good fit and our solution did not meet a customer's needs, I still considered it a win. Why would I consider it a win if we did not gain a new customer and new business? Well, if we followed our process, we would know with clarity that we did not meet the customer's needs, rather than second-guessing if we had missed something we should have learned in the sales process. With a clear understanding of the customer's needs, we may have uncovered an opportunity to refine and improve our solution.

Be mindful of the close rate (number of new customers gained divided by your total number of target customers), as it varies widely across different industries and is impacted not only by the effectiveness of your sales process but by your sales skills, the quality of the target customers, and your competition. Be realistic. A solid close rate is 20 to 25 percent. Think about it: If your goal is to gain ten new customers, you will need to have a quality target list of forty to fifty, demonstrating another reason for having a repeatable, systematic sales approach. It is a numbers game, and if you are going to raise your close rate, you will need to continuously improve the effectiveness of your sales approach.

Whether your startup is a one-time-sale business, a repeat business, or even an e-commerce business with little or no direct customer interaction, there is value in developing a repeatable, systematic sales approach with you as the owner leading your sales efforts. The value is in identifying your target customer needs and problem-solving through direct engagement and good communication. It leads to a better understanding of the customer, providing you with the knowledge you need to continuously improve your product or service along with the changing needs of the customer.

Time is money. Your time is just as valuable as your customer's time. Prepare with the purpose of being respectful of your customer's time and to make the most of your time. Take advantage of the selling opportunity with new customers. You and your startup will be better for it. You can do it!

Use the following checklist to help you stay organized with your progress.

HACK 9
ADD EXTERIOR ELEMENTS

Completed

Have you developed profile criteria for ideal customers? ☐

Did you compile a quality target customer list? ☐

Did you write down your company story? ☐

Have you put together effective open-ended questions to engage the customer? ☐

Are you prepared to move to the next phase of construction? ☐

HACK 10

FIT INTERIOR FINISHING DETAILS
Fund Your Startup

Ideas without capital are like seeds without soil. It's capital that turns business potential into business productivity.

— HENDRITH VANLON SMITH JR., INVESTOR AND CORPORATE ADVISOR

THE PROBLEM: I DON'T KNOW HOW TO FUND MY STARTUP

THE FINISHING DETAILS can make all the difference in whether a home is perceived as well-built and of high quality. Flaws in the finishing details may be perceived as a sign of broader construction flaws.

If your builder constructed a quality home but completely missed the mark on the fit and finishing details, you would see aesthetic issues from gaps, seams, and misalignment between materials. There would be functional problems such as windows, doors, and cabinets that do not work properly. Delays and overruns would extend project timelines, with rework adding additional materials and costs. As the buyer investing in a new home, you would quickly realize that these issues would compromise your confidence and have you questioning whether there were other construction flaws that you could not see and whether the new home was a good investment.

Funding your startup is like fitting the interior finish details of a home. Your startup may have a solid foundation, structure, and other elements needed for a quality build. However, if the details you present to a potential investor have gaps and flaws, this will compromise their confidence and decrease your chances of securing the necessary resources to launch and grow your new business.

If you cannot clearly explain key details like the problem and your solution, customer value proposition, market opportunity, and key competitors, you'll struggle to secure funding. You also need to articulate how your business operates, the team's strength that will make it happen, your financial projections, and how much money you need and why. Without effectively presenting these details, you cannot secure funding for your startup.

THE HACK: FIT INTERIOR FINISHING DETAILS

According to 2023 Census Bureau data, the most common source of business startup funding comes from personal or family savings. The primary reason for owners using personal savings is that it is the easiest, quickest, and most cost-effective way to fund their startup business. However, the downside is you are putting your personal finances at risk, and if the business fails, you could end up in debt.

You may need to overcome the following challenges when securing funding for your startup business:

- *Uncertain revenue and cash flow*: There is no track record of success or ability to show a solid revenue stream or cash flow.

- *Lack of collateral*: Startup businesses may have limited assets, making it difficult to secure traditional loans, especially if the asset is intellectual property and the value is difficult to determine.

- *Market and economic uncertainty*: Economic downturns, market fluctuations, and even world events can make it difficult to secure funding, with perceived higher risks from potential investors or lenders.

- *Owner inexperience*: As unfair as it may sound, investors and lenders make decisions based on assessing the owner's experience and expertise when they evaluate the startup business's potential for success.

- *Complexity in the process*: Navigating legal and lending agreements is a complex process and can be stressful when trying to understand the right decision and best path to fund your business.

Three basic types of funding are available. To decide which type of funding makes the most sense for your startup, it is a good idea to start by understanding the basics of each one, including advantages and disadvantages.

Debt is borrowing or acquiring a business loan. The advantage is that, as the owner, you do not have to give up any ownership in your business to get funding. The disadvantages are that you may have to pay a high interest rate, the loan term could be shorter than you prefer, and you will have to make regular loan payments, even if your business is not performing well.

Equity is selling ownership interest in your business. There are several types of equity investors, each with its own funding criteria. The advantage of selling equity is that you do not have to repay the investment. The disadvantage is that you give up some ownership and decision-making, depending on the involvement and requirements of the investor.

Two of the most common types of equity investors are angel investors and venture capitalists. Angel investors are wealthy individuals who invest their own money in promising startups. The upside is that they can provide sound business advice. The downside is that they typically want a significant stake in your business. Venture capitalists are professional investors who solicit different sources to collectively fund their investments. They typically make significant investments in high-growth startups and are directly involved in the business decisions. If you need a considerable investment, venture capital may make sense. The challenge with venture capitalists is that they tend to be aggressive and want a higher return in a short time frame, often pushing for quick growth and higher risks.

Grants are typically funding from the government or another organization. The advantage is that you do not have to pay back a grant. The disadvantage is that grants can be difficult to qualify for and, in most cases, are for nonprofits or businesses whose purpose is improving a cause for social well-being. Some local grants also come with substantial requirements to fulfill the grant conditions. Additionally, some organizations may request that their branding or logos be associated with your startup.

Startups and small businesses may wish to register for a UEI number (Unique Equity Identifier) if they plan to pursue federal grants. The UEI number system was created in 2022 to replace the Data Universal Numbering System (DUNS). The purpose of the UEI number is to more easily identify businesses that are eligible for federal grants, and it is required for small businesses that wish to seek and gain contracts with the federal government. There can be benefits at the state and local levels, as well. There is no cost to register, and it is not required if you intend to conduct business exclusively in the private sector. If you want to register your startup to acquire a UEI number, visit the System for Award Management.

Nail It:

To pursue funding for your startup, first do your research, create a solid pitch deck, know your numbers, and prepare accordingly.

WHAT YOU CAN DO TOMORROW

As you choose the type of funding that makes the most sense for your startup business, you can take action to determine the best fit to support the success of your new business.

- **Determine how much money you need.** Considering that when you start your business, you will have uncertain revenue and cash flow, it is important to clarify your monthly operating expenses while you grow sales, generate profit, and build cash to pay expenses. Operating expenses refer to the costs your business incurs from normal day-to-day activities to run the business. In Hack 5, we covered examples of operating expenses. Now, it is time to make a detailed list of operating expenses broken down into monthly increments.

Standard operating expenses:

▸ *Employee compensation and benefits* – remember to include yourself if needed

▸ *Administration and overhead* – rent or lease payments for facilities and equipment, utilities, and office supplies and equipment

▸ *Inventory* – the cost of both raw materials and the finished goods produced and maintained on hand for sale to customers

▸ *Marketing and advertising* – for promoting your business to potential customers

▸ *Professional services* – legal and accounting services

▸ *Taxes and licenses* – all business-related taxes and potential operating licenses

▸ *Insurances* – liability and workers compensation, plus property insurance

▸ *Travel and entertainment* – estimate of costs for engaging with prospective customers to generate sales

▸ *Contingencies* - include an amount for unplanned expenses such as repairs and maintenance

Nail It:

If your startup funding comes from a business loan, you must include bank payments with interest in your standard operating expenses. Consider listing your operating expenses as putting together a budget that adds up to the total amount of money you need to operate each month.

- **Understand your business model.** If you have a business model that requires significant funding for equipment, carrying an inventory of raw materials, and storing finished products, it makes more sense to find an equity partner in the form of an angel investor or venture capital firm. If you are starting a service business with less funding needed for equipment, raw materials, and supplies, you may be able to start with a smaller amount of funding in the form of a bank loan or line of credit.

- **Estimate how many months of operating expenses you need.** The number of months of operating expenses you need will answer this question: How many months will it take for your monthly sales and profits to cover your operating expenses? Estimating the number of months of operating expenses you need should be carefully considered. None of us can accurately predict the future. What you can do is consider the various factors and conditions that could impact the length of time it takes to grow sales, make a profit, and reach the point where you can pay your operating expenses without funding from an outside source. These factors and conditions include:

Your personal approach

> ▸ Are you aggressive in your approach and think you can scale up and grow quickly?

> ▸ Are you conservative in your approach and think it will take longer for your

sales to ramp up and reach the month when sales, profit, and cash can cover your monthly operating expenses?

Length of your sales cycle

▸ If you have a long sales cycle, such as selling to other businesses, it may take time to build a customer relationship and successfully acquire new customers and sales.

▸ If you have a short sales cycle, such as selling a product directly to consumers, the purchase transaction usually happens quickly. This allows you to collect sales dollars faster and cover monthly expenses sooner. However, there may still be a delay in completing a purchase transaction.

Significance of the market opportunity

▸ Your product or service may be in high demand in a fast-growing market where you believe sales will grow more quickly. You may be entering a more mature market where it may take longer to establish your brand and earn business from established competitors.

Advantages of your solution compared to competitors

▸ Does your product or service have clear advantages over competitors, such as a better solution, a better price, or better service that would allow you to grow sales more quickly? Is your solution more on par with competitors, meaning it may take longer to establish a solid customer base to grow sales?

Effectiveness of marketing and sales strategies

▸ How confident are you in the effectiveness of your marketing strategies to get the word out and generate interest and inquiry in your product or service? Do you believe your sales approach will support a solid close rate with target customers?

Economic conditions

▸ How the economy is performing can also impact how quickly you can grow sales. You do not have to become an economist, but understanding the basic indicators impacting the economy's health can provide valuable information about potential target customer behavior. Basic indicators include unemployment, inflation, current interest rates, consumer confidence index, retail sales behavior, and even the housing market.

- **Determine the risks and rewards.** Equity investors such as angel investors or venture capital firms will invest in high-risk businesses; however, they expect a high return if your business is successful. If you decide that a bank loan, credit card, or line of credit makes more sense, you will pay higher interest rates with shorter repayment terms, but they are easier to obtain, and you do not give up any ownership.

BUILDING MOMENTUM

Successfully securing funding for your startup requires an organized, well-thought-out presentation that you have researched, learned, accomplished, planned, calculated, and projected to instill confidence in a potential lender or investor that your startup will be a winner. Here are the sequential steps.

STEP 1: Calculate your financial projections.

Once you list and total your detailed monthly operating expenses, the next step is to estimate monthly sales and profit projections. Here's some good news: You already did the work in Hack 5 when you determined your profit potential and whether you were on the right track to make money and succeed.

Nail It:

Develop a pro forma. A pro forma is a financial calculation tool, such as a worksheet or spreadsheet, that helps calculate projections in business planning. If you are not familiar with a pro forma tool, work with your accountant or other well-versed financial businessperson to set up a pro forma specific to your startup. (See an example pro forma at ronneary.com.)

STEP 2: Decide on the type of funding for your startup.

Based on your financial projections and the months of funding you will need to cover operating expenses, decide on the ideal type of funding for your startup. In most cases, a combination of your savings and a business loan or line of credit will be sufficient to fund your startup. However, depending on your comfort level with the calculated finan-cial risk, finding an equity partner may make more sense. This decision is subjective, and your financial projections will give you insight into which type of funding is best for your situation.

STEP 3: Create a solid pitch deck.

A pitch deck lays out and presents your business, culmi-nating in asking for funding. Even if you are not seeking outside funding, a pitch deck is an excellent way to bring everything together for you, potential owners, and stake-holders to understand where the gaps are and gain align-ment on your vision, goals, and projects. Table 10.1 shows the elements of a pitch deck.

Elements of a Pitch Deck

Cover Page	Your logo and description of your business.
Problem Statement	Needs of the customer from the customer's perspective.
Solution	Your solution and how it meets the customer's needs and is different and better, stating your customer value proposition.
Market Opportunity	Overview of the industry and market trends. Detailed view of your target market segment and market position.
Business Model	How your business works (operates), from customer inquiry to product or service delivery, the customer experience, and how you will make money.
Milestones	Chronology of your accomplishments from Hacks 1–9.
Go-to-Market Strategy	Tactical marketing and sales strategies you have developed and are putting into action.
Key Competitors	Overview of key competitors and their size, duration in business, product or service offerings, and number of employees, plus your assessment of their strengths and weaknesses.
Team	Key team members and co-owners, with a short description of their relevant experience and unique strengths and skills they bring to advance the startup's success.
Financial Projections	Monthly increments on a pro forma to project how many months it will take for sales and profits to cover monthly expenses.
Funding Request	Amount of funding you are asking for and how you will use the funds.

Table 10.1

217

STEP 4: Know your numbers.

One of the first questions any investor, whether a business banking loan officer or equity investor, will ask is about your financial projections. You want to make sure you have a good understanding of your financial projections and your thought process on how you determined them. Knowing your numbers and effectively walking through them will convey confidence to the decision-maker of your funding request.

STEP 5: Practice presenting your pitch deck.

Securing funding for your startup involves selling your business idea, growth opportunity, and earnings potential. However, investors make subjective decisions based on assumptions and their degree of confidence in you and your startup's potential success. Once you complete your pitch deck, practice presenting it to colleagues, your accountant, and friends and family. You can also video record your presentation for review and improvement. Remember, you are asking for money; practice to present confidently.

STEP 6: Have a backup plan.

There is a chance that an investor will say no. Put together a list of alternatives just in case and be prepared to present to several investors to gain approval and secure funding. For example, if you are seeking a bank loan or line of credit, it makes sense to present your pitch deck to a few banks—not just to get approved for funding but also to shop for the best deal for the lowest loan interest rate. Whether you are presenting to an angel investor or venture capital firm, research them in detail before the meeting. The key is to find an equity investor you trust and can work with, considering they will have a stake in your new business.

REMOVING OBSTACLES

Many details, projections, and calculations go into determining how much money you will ask for to fund your startup. If you have worked through the details in Hacks 1–9, you should have all the information you need to create a solid pitch deck. However, here are some common concerns and how to address them.

What if I am unsure whether we can deliver on the projections? You will not be sure. I have used the phrase, "The projection (or forecast) is wrong before the ink dries." It may sound a bit ridiculous and make you question why you are doing all these calculations if they may be wrong. Think about Hack 6, where you established key objectives and success standards. Your projection becomes your goal, your success standard, and it will drive your motivation and execution.

Is there a standard amount of funding that is reasonable to request? It is reasonable to ask for twelve to eighteen months of operating expenses in your funding request. This should give you sufficient time to grow your sales from your marketing and sales strategies and focus on providing consistent, superb service to your new customers. Your projections may indicate a shorter time that you will work toward, but asking for a longer time period is a conservative approach and a reasonable request.

How can I avoid missing expenses in our monthly operating estimate? Most of us are not accountants or financial experts. Even if you are, it is a good practice to consult and work with a professional financial accountant to audit what you have accounted for in your monthly operating expenses. You can also adjust your contingency amount to cover any unplanned expenses.

How do I know I am getting a fair interest rate for my bank loan, line of credit, or business credit card? As a startup with no history, you do not have much leverage to negotiate better interest rates. If they seem unreasonable, research the fair market interest rate for the amount of funding you are requesting with similar loan terms and share it with your lender to attempt to secure a better rate. Also, remember to make any repayments early. Once you have built a solid repayment history and your business is growing profitably with solid cash flow, you will have some leverage to renegotiate and refinance your business loan at a better interest rate.

What if I lack the skills to assemble a professional-looking pitch deck? A pitch deck should be ten slides long, instill confidence, and be formatted professionally. Online tools and templates can help you with the layout and walk you through the steps to create a pitch deck. You can also find a colleague or friend who is skilled and tech-savvy to help you.

How do I capture the different tax amounts I must pay? I hear you—ugh, taxes. Business taxes are many, change regularly, and are complex. They include income tax, payroll tax, property tax, sales tax, federal tax, state tax, and local tax, and all are impacted by your business's legal structure. Consult a professional business tax accountant. Not complying with tax laws is not an option. A licensed business tax accountant is a required investment in your business and part of your monthly operating expenses.

THE HACK IN ACTION

Rachel has developed a unique and innovative idea into a potential business. She enjoys getting together with her friends regularly for conversations over glasses of fine wine. However, the bar and restaurant scene does not appeal to her and her friends. They have unsuccessfully tried to find a local place to go that is quiet and relaxing, where they can just sit in comfy chairs and enjoy casual conversation and each other's company.

Rachel's idea is to open a casual wine lounge called Vino Fino (Spanish for fine wine), where people can stop in with friends and buy bottles of wine to share and relax. Her idea evolved to include a well-designed, inviting space with a private room that could be rented out for small events or parties and a retail store. She was clear that her business would not be a restaurant but would offer a small menu of cheese plates and various charcuterie board selections to complement a bottle of wine. If the guests wanted a real meal, they would be welcome to bring in food, have it delivered to the wine lounge, or hire catering in the private party room.

After working with her financial accountant, calculating her profit potential, detailing the operating expenses, and projecting sales growth from her marketing and sales strategies, she determined that she would need funding to operate her business for approximately twenty-six months.

Taking a closer look at her marketing and sales strategies, she added the idea of hosting a monthly wine club. Members would join by subscription and receive two bottles of red and two bottles of white wine each month. She would select the winemaker and vintage, which would be different each month. This would help boost monthly sales and also more effectively manage the wine inventory for retail store sales in the lounge.

She also realized that the monthly wine club was an ideal marketing strategy for staying connected with customers by sending updates on wines and happenings at the Vino Fino lounge. Adding the monthly wine club cut the funding needed in half from twenty-six to thirteen months, so she thought it reasonable to ask for eighteen months of operating costs for peace of mind.

She outlined her business model as a product and service business with modest capital needs and reasonable monthly operating expenses, along with her intent to invest twenty thousand dollars in the business from her personal savings. She concluded that pursuing a business bank loan for funding made the most sense. She was conservative in her sales projections and operating costs and aware that she was a one-location, unique small business serving her local market. Rachel had a specific vision for her business and had no interest in taking on a partner, affirming that a bank loan and business credit card would be her best avenues to secure funding.

Through her research of potential competitors and other options in the area, she was confident that the innovative approach of Vino Fino was a better option for friends to get together over glasses of fine wine.

After her detailed work in Hacks 1–9 to research, learn, and work through the steps to define her business, from market analysis to marketing and sales strategies, she had all the information she needed to create the pitch book.

She targeted three banks and secured a business loan for the eighteen months of operating expenses she requested to launch Vino Fino.

You've done much work to build your startup from the ground up. You are organized and clearly understand the market, market opportunities, and market position of your new business, the unique value your solution brings to target customers, and the profit potential of your product or service. You navigated the process to decide on your legal structure and came up with an ideal name for your business.

You have meticulously laid out the day-to-day work and needed resources, and you have set solid goals to push yourself and your team to succeed with top-notch service to your customers. The marketing strategies you developed will get the word out about your new business, and you are confident in executing your sales approach and reaching out to prospective target customers.

After completing your pitch deck, how would you answer the questions originally proposed in Hack 5:

- Am I on the right track?

- Will I make money?

- Does my new business have a chance of succeeding?

If you answered "yes" to these three questions, then you have done the detailed work to launch your startup.

It's time to map your critical path and take action

A critical path is the sequence of tasks that must be completed to open for business. The goal is to complete everything collectively to meet your desired launch date. Start with making a checklist of everything that must be done, the anticipated time to complete each task, and who is responsible for each task. This list should include the lead time for receiving raw materials, supplies, or equipment and the time it will take to implement marketing strategies to get the word out about your new business.

The longest task will determine whether your launch date is realistic or needs to be adjusted. There may be some flexibility, such as with shorter, simple tasks where you can delay the start and still meet your target launch date. Be mindful that some tasks depend on the completion of others and need priority attention to complete them and move to the next task. A good example is your company logo. It will be represented across many elements of your business: your website, social media presence, print materials such as business cards and company brochures, technical documents, and packaging. All these elements have different timelines to complete, so finalize your logo first.

Early in my career, I worked as a product and project manager and learned that having a critical path kept me on schedule and on top of all the tasks I had to complete to launch a new product. The critical path helped me manage my time effectively and stay on task. It also helped me when the critical path was shared by enlisting accountability for others with completion dates for specific tasks, including suppliers, marketing designers, and employees who owned different aspects of the project.

Time is money

Once you secure funding, you have two valuable inter-connected resources: time and money. I firmly believe in doing everything with a sense of urgency once I am clear and confident in the direction and plan. I become consumed with completing projects and tasks on time, on budget, and on schedule. Those who have worked with me might use words like "pushy," "aggressive," "obsessed," and sometimes even "unrealistic."

Time is money, and as a business owner, you must push and do everything with a sense of urgency to be successful and reach the milestone month when your sales and profits cover your operating expenses. I hope you do it ahead of your projections.

Congratulations!

You have just completed your business plan by working through the Hacks to launch your startup.

The next page shows a checklist to help you stay organized with your progress.

HACK 10
FIT INTERIOR
FINISHING DETAILS

Completed

Have you captured and totaled your monthly estimated operating expenses?

Did you determine the months of operating expenses you will need to cover?

Did you utilize a pro forma worksheet to calculate financial projections?

Did you decide on the type of funding that makes sense for your startup?

Did you complete your pitch deck?

Are you prepared to move to the next phase of construction?

HACK 11

PASS THE FINAL INSPECTION
Accurately Track Your Results

*Accounting is the language of business.
The more accurately it's spoken, the more
likely the business is to succeed.*

— H. ROSS PEROT SR., BUSINESSMAN AND PHILANTHROPIST

THE PROBLEM: INACCURATE TRACKING GENERATES NEGATIVE OUTCOMES

AFTER MANY DECISIONS and much work and coordination, the final step in building a new home is passing the final inspection. Failing the final inspection can have far-reaching financial and operational consequences. The project may undergo rework and corrections, additional labor and materials costs, and delays in financing. Lenders may withhold final payments or funding until the project passes inspection, compromising the builder's cash flow.

What's more, legal and compliance issues will inevitably arise from code violations, resulting in penalties and fines. Time lost, damage to the builder's reputation, and stress from the corrections are not good.

Similarly, inaccurate financial tracking and accounting will result in negative outcomes for your new business. The difference between a successful business and a struggling one often comes down to how well it manages its finances.

In the short term, you risk being unable to determine your business's month-to-month health. This lack of awareness leads to reactive decision-making to address immediate financial challenges, operational disruptions from inventory shortages, or product delays that impact customer service and satisfaction. One of the most damaging impacts is the loss of confidence from customers, employees, investors, or other stakeholders.

Long-term risks manifest as errors with legal and regulatory consequences, such as tax liability from incorrect financial calculations and non-compliance with legal business reporting standards, leading to fines, penalties, or legal actions. Incorrect financial reporting can also lead to poor decision-making on strategic topics such as pricing strategies, investing too much in inventory or equipment, and not having the cash flow to meet operating expenses such as payroll, vendor invoices, or loan repayments.

THE HACK: PASS THE FINAL INSPECTION

Accurately tracking inbound and outbound money transactions for your business, complying with tax requirements, and calculating financials are not only necessary but also required by law.

Structuring proper accounting processes involves working with a certified public accountant (CPA). Unless you are an accountant, this is a must. A seasoned CPA can guide you through the details and recommend the right tools, such as accounting software and a payroll resource, and help you establish a schedule of activities to complete on time to stay current and accurate.

Also, accurately identifying and capturing the different transaction activities during the month will help your accountant prepare an accurate monthly profit and loss (P&L) statement, which will give you a month-to-month snapshot of your financial situation.

Beyond the required legal accounting compliance, a monthly P&L provides the key information you need to adjust as needed and make the best decisions to manage your business successfully.

WHAT YOU CAN DO TOMORROW

- **Open a business bank account.** To keep business and personal finances separate, open separate bank accounts for your business. If you will be receiving customer payments by credit card, you can work with your bank to have payments deposited directly into your business banking account.

- **Find and hire a trusted CPA.** Interview a few reputable CPA firms to find the one you are most confident in working with. Share a general list of areas where you will need administration and regular support to qualify their capabilities and understand general monthly costs. Examples include bookkeeping, payables, receivables, expense tracking, payroll, cash flow, financial reporting, and tax management.

- **Work with your attorney to draft a confidentiality agreement.** It is generally a good idea to have a confidentiality agreement in place with your business accountant to protect sensitive information about your business. The primary purpose is to maintain trust and confidence in the relationship. Additionally, you want to be able to share all financial details with your accountant so they can be the most effective at supporting your business. A confidentiality agreement should include the type of information you wish to protect, the duration of the agreement, and the consequences if it is breached.

Nail It:

Many reputable accounting firms will automatically include a confidentiality agreement in their proposal to work with you, as they are equally motivated to have the most open and effective working relationship with their clients. This could save you money by not having to work with an attorney to draft one.

BUILDING MOMENTUM

It's time to outline and identify the different transactions and financial operating tasks, their frequency, completion deadlines, and who is responsible for each task. Staying on schedule will support the timely completion of the monthly P&L and your business tax liabilities.

STEP 1: Outline the chart of accounts (COA) and general ledger (GL) codes.

Determining these financial details may feel overwhelming if the process is new to you, but you will get the hang of it soon, and your CPA will guide you through the process. Think of it as a catalog system for your financial transactions.

A chart of accounts is part of standard accounting practices. It is a list of all the items within your business that you need to record and organize as financial transactions to accurately generate financial reports, such as the P&L statement and the balance sheet. A balance sheet is a summary of assets, liabilities, and equity and is another financial tool used to evaluate financial health, liquidity, solvency, and future cash flows.

Chart of accounts examples:

- *Assets*: Resources a company owns

- *Liabilities*: Obligations or debts a company owes

- *Equity*: Owner's interest in the company

- *Income*: Money a business earns

- *Expenses*: Costs incurred by the business to operate

General ledger codes are the numeric codes and unique identifiers assigned under each account in the chart of accounts. Think of them as a shorthand method for organizing and categorizing the different financial transactions. As the owner with the best understanding of your operations and knowledge of the transactions in your business, your role involves working with your accountant to define the meaning of the numeric code categorized under each account in the chart of accounts.

General ledger numeric codes still fall under standard accounting practices, but by defining their meanings, you can customize them to the specific needs of your business type, industry, and structure. This will make it easier for you to identify, organize, and track your unique financial transactions.

STEP 2: Develop a schedule of when you must complete accounting tasks.

Make a list of the accounting tasks and a schedule of the frequency and deadline to complete them. Examples of typical accounting tasks include recording sales and purchase transactions, invoicing customers, processing accounts receivables and payables, running payroll, tracking and logging business expenses, receiving materials into inventory, completing cycle counts of material in inventory to ensure accuracy, and other financial transactions that may be specific to your type of business.

STEP 3: Choose the right accounting software.

Many accounting software tools are available, and I do not recommend a particular one. Most accounting software programs for small businesses today are cloud-based (over the internet) and secure with user logins, and user-level access is based on roles. The cost is typically a subscription model that depends on the number of users and functions needed, making it affordable for small businesses. One of the most used tools is Intuit QuickBooks, which is familiar to almost all CPAs who work with small businesses. Accounting software tools offer flexibility, security, and broad functionality to manage workflow processes and generate business intelligence reports.

Nail It:

Your business accountant will be a valuable resource for recommending the best accounting software to manage your business. Provide your accountant with a comprehensive overview of your business, operational framework, team structure, and responsibilities to give them a full understanding of your accounting needs. Share your pitch deck to give them the full scope of your business plan and how you will operate.

STEP 4: Learn the accounting system.

User training is available with most accounting system software providers, and your bookkeeper or accountant is also a resource. Commit to training for yourself and your team members who will use the software. Remember: "Know-how will always outdo guess-how." It is better to learn how to effectively use accounting software and enter transactions correctly than it is to make repeated errors and spend time making corrections.

REMOVING OBSTACLES

It can be challenging to stay on top of the timeliness and accuracy of recording financial transactions for your business, especially when your work hours are divided between your regular day-to-day activities and time spent reacting to customer inquiries, employee questions, and issues or problems that you must prioritize and address. Here are common questions about accurately tracking your results, and my guidance.

What if I make mistakes entering transactions? Accounting systems have been described as "garbage in, garbage out." Accuracy is critical, but errors will be made, and they can be corrected. Be selective in choosing who will have access to your system. Limit access based on team member roles and responsibilities. Also, if someone on your team is not process-driven and does not have the best attention to detail, they probably should not have system access or conduct accounting tasks. Your book-keeper or accountant will be able to troubleshoot and make corrections, but this can get expensive if it is a regular occurrence.

Nail It:

If you recognize that a transaction mistake has been made, it is better to reach out to your accountant or bookkeeper the first time to get it corrected rather than try to correct it yourself. Have them walk through how they corrected it so you can learn how to fix it should it happen again.

How can I find the time to enter the financial transactions? You need to focus on selling and growing your business. It may make sense to outsource recording financial transactions by hiring a bookkeeper. There are advantages to hiring a bookkeeper: expertise and experience, accuracy and reliability, cost and time savings, and the peace of mind that accounting tasks are being completed correctly and on time. Please be aware that you will still need to accurately identify the transactions and effectively communicate them to your bookkeeper for entry into the accounting system.

Can I get by without paying a CPA to oversee my accounting? Hiring a CPA is a wise investment with many benefits, including expertise and accuracy, financial insights and business advice, compliance and tax planning, and more time for you to focus on driving your business. If you decide not to work with a CPA to help manage the financial aspects of your startup, then maybe starting and running a new business is not for you.

Is a confidentiality agreement necessary? Only you can answer this question. If you have a unique business with ownership of intellectual property, product, or process innovations that you feel are competitive advantages for your business and need to be protected, it is appropriate to require a confidentiality agreement with your CPA and any other business you work with that could have access to confidential information related to your company.

THE HACK IN ACTION

Harper had always been known for her impeccable style and eye for fashion. She graduated from college with a double major in fashion merchandising and fashion styling. She loved designing jewelry and was on top of the latest trends in metals, colors, and gemstones, plus how to bring them all together to create elegant designs. Harper worked as an assistant manager at an upscale women's clothing store, and she enjoyed her job, but with her passion for style and interest in creating jewelry, she wanted to do more.

She designed a line of jewelry and created an e-commerce jewelry side business called gemifyboutique.com. Her niche designs included layered necklaces, bracelets, and earrings in mix-and-match metals and various materials, including silver, rose gold, white gold, black enamel, gemstones, and modern pearls. She also created some bold, oversized designs.

Harper found quality suppliers for components—one in China, two in the United States, and a unique gem supplier in Canada. Her products shown on her online digital storefront were assembled after customers placed orders from her supply of components, and she shipped directly to the customers. Her website was equipped for automated e-commerce where customers select the product, put it in their cart, place the order, and pay by credit card. Jewelry is small, lightweight, and easy to ship. She would assemble the pieces in her condo and hired two part-time employees to gather orders, pack them up, and label them for shipping. She was even able to coordinate with UPS to pick up orders so she did not have to take them to a UPS location to be shipped.

She opened a business account with her bank, which approved her for a small-business loan and a credit card for business expenses and purchases of the different components to make her jewelry. Her banker recommended a couple of accounting firms to help her set up and correctly manage all the financial transactions for both buying and selling.

One of the accounting firms she contacted was highly experienced in working with small e-commerce businesses and asked her what her primary concerns were with managing the financial transactions. Harper shared that she needed an efficient and accurate way to manage purchases and track the inventory of the different components (some of the gemstones and gold and silver chains were expensive), administer payroll to her part-time employees, handle accounting for sales tax, and reconcile the online sales with credit card payments. They set up the chart of accounts and, with her input, established the general ledger codes that lined up with her workflow of financial transactions. They recommended keeping things simple, considering that she still held a full-time job, and said it may make sense to have a bookkeeper reconcile the day-to-day transactions. She knew she was not an accountant, so she agreed, and they outlined the recommended schedule of tasks that the bookkeeper would execute to reconcile purchases and sales with payments, administer payroll on a weekly schedule, track inventory, and connect directly once a week to review open items.

The accountant recommended QuickBooks as her accounting software. It was their standard for many years, and their bookkeeper was an expert in it as well. The software was cloud-based, and they would only need three logins: for Harper, her accountant, and, of course, the bookkeeper. She did have to upgrade the subscription to accommodate e-commerce, but it was still affordable and within her budget. Payroll was included in the software, and all she had to do was send an email each week to inform her bookkeeper of how much to pay each part-time employee.

Harper was concerned about tracking and managing her inventory and understanding her cash flow so that she could cover her expenses, buy replacement components, and add new jewelry designs.

She had over four hundred components to make all the jewelry designs in her online store. Her accountant and bookkeeper shared with her that because the purchase transaction was by credit card, the money paid by the customer would be deposited into her bank account by the credit card companies within twenty-four hours of completing each transaction. This was great news. They proposed that if the bookkeeper had access to her online banking inbound and outbound financial transactions, they could be reconciled easily, and she would have regular, accurate updates on current cash flow. The accounting firm had banking access with other e-commerce businesses, so they adjusted their template confidentiality agreement to serve the needs of Harper, the bookkeeper, and the firm.

She worked with her accountant to set up and track the component items when they were made into necklaces, bracelets, and earrings. The accounting software could manage and track all of the details. Harper needed to provide them with all the jewelry items she would offer and a list of the specific components to assemble each one.

Harper wanted to get regular updates on what items and styles were popular, so she asked to get set up with a weekly sales report broken down by the different style categories to help her make the best decisions about new designs she might like to create. Working with the bookkeeper made her comfortable that the financial transactions would be managed accurately and on time, allowing her to focus on digital marketing strategies and work with her suppliers to buy exciting new jewelry-making components to create new designs. She would receive a prepared monthly financial profit and loss statement to show how much money she had made for the month; her accountant would review it with her and answer any questions about the month's financial activities.

Working with a reputable CPA and a bookkeeper to structure and manage the financial elements of a small business is a no-brainer. I am not an accountant, don't play one on TV, and have no desire to be one. I have always been eager to review the monthly P&L to see how we are doing, but I get frustrated when things do not make sense or when I find mistakes.

I was not good at being a bookkeeper and doing the "administrative" work that had to be done by someone. As a result, I used to make mistakes, procrastinate, and think my time could be better spent focused on marketing, sales, working with customers, improving operations, and driving the business. However, I learned that I needed to commit to the administrative work and identify transactions on schedule if I wanted an accurate and informative monthly P&L. I also needed to hire an accountant and a bookkeeper.

Your accountant and bookkeeper are there to properly track and translate your startup's financial activities, giving you a monthly money view of your business and providing information to make good decisions.

Use the following checklist to help you stay organized with your progress.

HACK 11

PASS THE FINAL INSPECTION

Completed

Have you opened a business banking account? ☐

Did you find a trusted CPA? ☐

Did you and your CPA outline a chart of accounts and general ledger codes? ☐

Did you and your CPA set a schedule for the completion of accounting tasks? ☐

Have you completed user training for your accounting software? ☐

Are you prepared to move to the next phase of construction? ☐

HACK 12

SETTLE INTO YOUR NEW HOME
Learn a Better Way

The secret of change is to focus all your energy not on fighting the old, but on building the new.

— DAN MILLMAN, COACH, AUTHOR, AND LECTURER

THE PROBLEM: RESISTANCE TO CHANGE BLOCKS PROGRESS

FROM THE INITIAL design to passing the final inspection, you have been involved in every detail of building your new home. After all the planning, preparation, coordination, and construction, it is time to settle into your new home. However, you recognize that moving in comes with its own set of challenges to solve.

What's different from the construction process is that you must now solve issues by working on them independently. These activities may include organizing different spaces and storage areas, and adjusting to new room layouts, a new neighborhood, a new commute to work, and a new set of local stores. There may also be budgeting changes in utility bills, the mortgage, landscape maintenance or snow removal, and unexpected appliance or mechanical repairs.

What if you resisted the opportunity to adjust and improve even the smallest details, such as where to position the coffee maker on the kitchen counter or how to reposition furniture for a better flow or room layout? Your new home would fall short of being a better, more efficient living space because of your resistance to adjustments and improvements.

The same truth applies to the business you are building. Now that you have done all the work from planning to launching your new business, what would happen if you resisted change once you are up and running? The result would be a lack of progress in interacting with customers, processing orders, deploying effective marketing strategies, and mastering your sales approach.

Resistance or apathy to learn a better way will block progress and the opportunity for improvement in *all* of your business areas. With the speed of change in today's business world, your new business would fall short of its potential at best, and fail at worst.

Resistance to change is your reluctance to adjust based on what you believe your business should be. Add the fear of failure, and the reluctance to change increases rather than decreases. We do not initiate change if we are not confident in our ability to adapt to it. Resistance to change is the enemy of a startup business.

THE HACK: SETTLE INTO YOUR NEW HOME

Your passion, creativity, strategic thinking, sound business approach, and attention to detail have helped you work through all the Hacks to develop a business plan and launch your business. *Now* is the time to be mindful of these three lessons as you figure out a better way and drive toward success: learning never stops, change is constant, and continuous improvement is, well, continuous.

The primary advantage of a startup business is the steep early learning curve combined with the agility to make changes, adjustments, and improvements. Having an open and curious mind for learning and finding a better way will lead to creativity and innovation.

WHAT **YOU** CAN DO TOMORROW

- **Learn by doing.** As a small-business owner, be a student of your work. Learn to perform every operational job function in your business effectively. You'll find immediate and future benefits, including:

  ▸ *Establishing the work standard.* When you are hands-on, you gain valuable insight into what is possible and should

---

be expected as the quality standard for repeatable tasks in each job function.

▸ *Serving as a backup.* If you have employees, you must be able to serve as the backup for almost every role in your new business and fill in if an employee is absent.

▸ *Adding flex capacity.* Early on, incoming business may be inconsistent. When help is needed to meet deadlines, you can add extra capacity to ensure the delivery of your products and services is complete and on time for customers.

▸ *Knowing future job descriptions.* If you need to hire a new employee for a specific job function as your business grows, you will be in a great position to create the job description, responsibilities, and expectations for standards of quality and capacity for the roles.

• **Get yourself a whiteboard.** Yes! Get yourself a whiteboard, and don't forget the box of multicolor dry-erase markers. My past teammates and business colleagues would say,

"There he goes again!" I am a huge fan of whiteboards and think they are one of the most effective business tools you can invest in. Two heads are better than one, and as a new business owner, you constantly trouble-shoot to find a better way. It's energizing and productive to conduct a seemingly spontaneous meeting utilizing a white-board. A whiteboard is such a simple visual tool that I regret not having a couple of them hanging on my wall earlier in my career for most planned and impromptu meetings and discussions.

Whiteboards have endless valuable ben-efits, such as increasing engagement and participation, capturing details while guiding the discussion, fostering creativity and clarity, solving problems and planning, and capturing the next steps and who is respon-sible for what. A whiteboard is simple and flexible, a must for any business to drive con-tinuous improvement.

Nail It:

As the owner and leader, always be the "scribe." You can capture and organize key details. It is also easier for you to guide the discussion, ask for clarification when writing a concept on the board from your team, and maintain focus on the topic.

- **Understand your strengths.** Understanding our strengths (and weaknesses) helps us work more effectively with each other by matching our work with our strengths and maximizing the value of our contributions to our company's success. I have been described as a "strength-based" people leader. Early in my career, my performance reviews focused on improving on my shortcomings and poor execution of some assigned tasks and areas of responsibility. There were plenty of them. Sometimes, I improved and met the work standard for my role. Sometimes, I continued to struggle and did not improve. I eventually realized I would never excel at tasks and responsibilities that exposed my weaknesses.

What's more, I did not like the tasks I was poor at, and even more telling is that my motivation and engagement were very low.

It made me think that I should try to figure out my strengths, and maybe by understanding them, I could align my strengths with job functions where I would perform much better. I still had challenges, but my plan to understand my strengths worked. I was much more effective and made more valuable contributions to the business's success. As my experience and responsibilities grew, I recognized that for the business areas and tasks I was not good at, I should have a member of my team or someone else with strength in that area take the lead.

I highly recommend that you invest the time for you and your team to take the Gallup CliftonStrengths assessment. The Gallup assessment identifies your five most dominant strengths. Over thirty-one million people have taken the assessment over the past twenty-five years, and my teams and I have found that it is incredibly accurate in identifying individual strengths and talents. (Note: Gallup CliftonStrengths is a registered trademark of Gallup, Inc.)

BUILDING MOMENTUM

Now that you are in the early growth stage, you're getting daily real-time feedback on your processes and customer experiences. The real value of that feedback is in what you decide to do with it to continuously improve. *Continuous improvement is an endless effort to learn a better way.* Here are the steps to build the momentum for success.

STEP 1: Inspect what you expect.

Perform early and frequent audits on your processes and review the quality of work from your team and yourself. In Hack 7, you defined and developed standard processes for your startup, and now that your business is in the early growth stage, audit and document those processes to determine what you may have missed, compare reality with your expectations, and assess what you can improve in your communications, your product or service quality, and your customers' experience.

Keep your vendors on their toes in the early growth stage, as well. Their quality and service are critical and directly connected to the success of your business. Monitor and hold the vendors accountable for their commitment to the quality of their products, services, and communication in support of your new business.

STEP 2: Establish multiple customer feedback loops.

I requested customer feedback several times during a steep learning curve with a new product line. One customer's feedback and suggestions were instrumental in expanding the product offering. Ultimately, she got what she wanted for a future project, and we improved the product line's overall design. The following are four easy-to-administer customer feedback loops to keep you engaged with customers and continuously improve the customer experience.

- **Customer surveys** are a common way to gather consistent, structured feedback on specific elements of the customer experience. A basic survey structure includes closed-ended questions with a rating scale (1–5 or 1–10) from poor to excellent, open-ended questions to capture customer thoughts, and identifier questions to learn customer profile information. It should be short and to the point. Remember, customers are investing their time and taking the survey as a courtesy.

  Examples of general customer satisfaction survey questions:

  On a scale of 1 to 5, with 1 being the worst and 5 being the best:

  ► How satisfied are you with the quality of our product or service?

  ► How likely are you to recommend us to a friend or colleague?

  ► How easy was it to navigate our website and find what you were looking for?

- ▶ How did our team perform in promptly answering all your questions?

- ▶ Overall, how would you rate your experience with our company?

Examples of open-ended feedback questions:

- ▶ How did you find us?

- ▶ What could we do to improve our product or service?

- ▶ What could we do to improve your experience in working with us?

Last, collect customer profiles and demographic information. Examples are age, sex, education level, profession, job title, and social media participation preferences. There are different thoughts on whether you should make the collection of this information required or optional. I prefer to make it required and state to the recipient that the information will provide us with the details we need to improve their customer experience.

Nail It:

Popular e-marketing tools include survey templates, which make it easy to set up and administer your customer satisfaction survey and compile results.

- **Social media interactions** are excellent avenues to actively engage with customers and gather feedback on their perceptions of your brand and how easy it is to work with your company, provide answers to their product and technical questions, share best practices, and request their thoughts about a new product or service before you launch it. I recommend starting by creating a private social media group (for example, on Facebook or LinkedIn). You can send a link to chosen participants and ask them to join. The value of these groups lies in their engagement with each other and your business.

Nail It:

If you decide that social media interaction is a good tool to engage customers, remember that it is not about selling or marketing your products or services; it is about getting their constructive input and feedback to help you improve. Be prepared to engage regularly and take action based on their suggestions for improvement.

- **Covert customer experience audits** or "secret shoppers" involve setting up a friend or colleague to pose as a customer and walk through the entire customer experience, from the initial contact to the final delivery of your product or service. Then, you audit their experience and address gaps or refine areas that help you continuously improve the customer journey.

- **Direct customer interviews** are one-on-one conversations with customers. There is no greater compliment to a customer than being contacted directly by the company owner to inquire and respectfully ask for their input and feedback on their experience in working with the company. Think about it: How many electronic customer surveys do you receive after making a purchase? A call or conversation is a more substantial investment of your time, but the return is substantially more valuable.

Nail It:

Include open-ended specific questions in your direct customer interview so you will get more specific and valuable responses. Then send a follow-up email to thank them for their time and feedback.

STEP 3: Push creativity over capital.

Creativity over capital is one of my favorite approaches for early-stage business growth (really for any business at any stage). Too often, business leaders look to two resources to solve a problem or improve a business function: people and money. For a new business, money is often tight, so when you cannot afford the additional money and people resources, you must get creative. This approach also fosters an ultra-focused, low-cost, problem-solving culture. As Amazon founder Jeff Bezos said, "Frugality breeds innovation."

You can often take advantage of cost-effective and free (yes, free) resources to address problems or improve a business function. Vendor resources and expertise are often available at no cost. They want you to succeed so you can buy more of their products or services, and utilizing their expertise is a value they can provide to you at a low cost to them. In most cases, it's only an investment of their time, plus it brings them value to learn and engage with you as the customer for ideas on how they can improve.

Trading services and sharing resources with other businesses are also methods of minimizing costs and driving efficiencies.

Members of trade organizations can also serve as resources for collaboration since they are actively working in the same market and industry and often face the same challenges. By sharing perspectives, best practices, and lessons learned from trial and error, you can accelerate your improvement and success.

STEP 4: Find a trusted advisor.

As an over-the-hill hockey player, I love playing with better, faster, more talented, and mostly younger players. They push me to play better and make better decisions. Well, I like to think I play better. I do find myself playing smarter. I am in a better position on the ice, more focused on making accurate passes, and able to see plays developing more clearly. They push me and energize me, leading by example with little or nothing being said, and I try to follow.

Find a trusted advisor, an accomplished entrepreneur, or a successful business leader with the experience and wisdom to challenge your thinking, provide sound advice, and push you to be a better version of yourself today than yesterday.

Give careful consideration when seeking an advisor or mentor. A friend or family member may not be the best choice, even though they know you well and you have mutual trust. Sure, you want to find someone you can trust; however, that person must also have business competence, expertise, and a willingness to challenge you.

- Consider the skills, knowledge, and experiences you want to develop.

- Look within your network and ask for referrals.

- Participate in industry events, online forums, or LinkedIn groups where experienced business professionals share their perspectives.

- Reach out directly and share your interest in learning from others.

An advisor or mentor relationship should include mutual benefits. Offer assistance where you may be of value, such as a fresh perspective on a project or business challenge they are experiencing. Be patient and respectful of their time, and share your appreciation for their perspective. Finally, stay in touch and share your progress based on their counsel and advice.

STEP 5: Embrace technology tools and AI.

Tech tools and AI applications are constantly upgrading and improving their features, capabilities, speed, and ease of use. If deployed properly, they can often improve a business's overall performance and success.

At the most basic level, the value of technology tools is efficiency. Technology allows small businesses to do more with fewer resources, saving time and money. Like staying current on your industry and market, you'll want to keep current on new technologies that may offer you a competitive advantage.

Many of us are at the beginning of the learning curve when it comes to understanding the potential and limitless possibilities of using AI—not just in our businesses but in our lives. With both positive and negative perspectives on how to use (or not use) AI, one thing is certain: The cognitive revolution has arrived. As AI evolves, routine tasks will be minimized with lower costs and improved efficiencies.

The use of AI has the potential to accelerate the three lessons that resonate throughout *Your Small Business Blueprint*:

1. Learning never stops.

2. Change is constant.

3. Continuous improvement is, well, continuous.

Through accelerating research and your learning, AI has the very real potential to enhance productivity and customer service in your evolving new business.

Keep it simple to start; sign up for a free version of an AI chat tool and use it as a virtual advisor to ask any business question or problem you need to solve. ChatGPT (GPT stands for General Purpose Technology) is an easy-to-use choice.

Nail It:

Be cautious about accepting responses from AI tools as entirely accurate or correct. Avoid letting AI make decisions for you. Instead, use the information provided as a source of insight and perspective while *you* evaluate the best course of action for your business.

REMOVING OBSTACLES

You will encounter challenges as you learn a better way. You are in the early growth stage and may not have enough repetition in your tasks or meaningful customer feedback to warrant making positive changes. Poor communication among your team can also contribute to missed opportunities for incremental or breakthrough improvements. Here are common obstacles and how to navigate them.

Why should I make changes so soon if I just launched my business? In Hack 7, you developed your standard processes and operational framework. They were well-thought-out plans, but once you put them into practice, you were immediately in evaluation, measurement, and improvement mode. In most cases, minor adjustments drive continuous improvement.

What if customers don't respond to feedback requests? To improve responses and the quality of feedback, you can motivate customers by offering an incentive, such as a small gift card, a coupon for a discount on a future purchase, or even money.

How do I proceed if I don't have the money to make the changes in the best way? The idea is to make incremental improvements. However, during a business's early growth stage, the best way may not be in the budget. Do not risk doing nothing because you find obstacles to doing it the best way. Best can be the enemy of better.

What if I do not have the physical skills to "learn by doing" every work task? We are all made differently and may have limitations in physically performing some tasks. Do not compromise your health and safety to learn by doing. The next best option is to identify who does a task best and learn by observation. Gather input from the person performing the task, ask questions, document steps, video record the task, and track the time it takes to complete. With these details, you can set the standard for successful completion and assess and identify areas for incremental improvements.

How do I respond if our vendors are not meeting their commitments? It can be tricky to hold vendors accountable when you are a new business and have not yet established the potential value that your business can bring to their company. Most vendors will likely prioritize larger, more established customers if they must choose. You can press them to meet their commitments to you, but this may have minimal success at enlisting accountability, even if you have a written agreement. You can talk openly about their challenges and ask what you can do differently to get what you need from the vendor when you need it.

During the COVID pandemic, our new business had to change some areas that I did not think we should have to adjust. However, the negative impact of the pandemic on the supply chain forced us to think differently, act differently, and find a way to work with our vendors to get what we needed, when we needed it, to best support our customers. Unknown impacts may be out of your control and your vendor's control. Just because you are the customer does not automatically enlist their accountability and drive their actions to prioritize supporting your business at any cost. Talk openly and creatively to find alternative solutions to work together for mutual benefit.

Nail It:

Negotiating your buy price from a vendor can be difficult, considering you are a new business. Approach negotiations with vendors in good faith, transparency, and respect, seeking mutual benefit. If you ask your vendor to be a low-price provider, ask them what you can do to be a low-cost customer. You may not be their largest customer, but you can share your motivation to be their best customer.

What if my team is not motivated to improve or find a better way? Generating energy around motivation for continuous improvement differs from setting expectations and success standards for employees. As the owner, *you* must establish a culture to find better ways of working.

Conduct a team huddle to review and discuss a specific task. Ask for input on how to make it better, faster, or produce a higher-quality output. Employees love to share their thoughts and perspectives if asked. We all feel valued when we contribute, so be inclusive when problem-solving. Just because you are the boss does not mean you are the expert in every area. Recognize and acknowledge individual strengths and enable each team member to contribute.

How do I know if we are improving? Remember that in Hack 5, we learned that nothing can be improved upon if it cannot be measured. Before you can measure, you must first establish a baseline standard of what it means to successfully complete a task. Once the baseline standard is established, then you can take the approach of *"We can beat that!"*

THE HACK IN ACTION

Let's revisit Mike and Tim from Hacks 2 and 6 with their new form of barnwood wall and ceiling products that they would ship to customers nationwide. Mike became the managing partner for the business, leading the day-to-day operations. In this role, he created and developed all operational and technical elements of the company.

Reviewing the business's strategy with its unique identity (market position) and CVP will help us understand Mike's goals and drive to learn a better way, innovate, and continuously improve in the early stages of business growth.

Goals for the business:

- Provide world-class, market-leading customer service to every influencer in the process, from design to buying decision to delivery.

- Streamline the supply chain and order-to-delivery process, and ship project orders directly from our warehouse to any job site in the country within five to seven business days.

- Ship samples the same day upon request by anyone involved in the project, at no charge.

- We will be an expert resource on any and all questions related to product specifications, project design, and installation.

- Ship orders complete and deliver on time to customers.

- *CVP: We will provide the best products, the best price, and the best service for our customers.*

When the business launched, the marketing strategies began to bring in prospective customers through quote requests from their website. Mike was the only operations employee at first, and he could manage the light volume and respond to customers with a total delivered price and all the details within an hour. As the owner, one of his roles was as the lead salesperson. He was in constant communication with customers, gathering feedback on improving service, how to provide quotes and information more clearly and effectively, filling sample requests, addressing installation questions, coordinating deliveries, and learning other details about what was most important to their purchase decision.

Mike worked fast and was organized, accurate, and efficient, and he ensured they met the goals in their unique market position and customer value proposition. The volume reached a level where Mike had to add additional sales team members in customer service, packing, and shipping orders.

He completed every task and job, from the initial contact with the customer to loading the order onto the delivery truck. In doing so, he learned that while the established startup processes were sound and worked for him, they would need to improve different tasks to do them more efficiently, consistently, and accurately, especially after adding and training additional employees.

There were four key areas where learning a better way was a must if they were to continue building on their best service goal to support their customers, outperform their competitors, and successfully grow the business.

At the time, too many calculations had to be made to determine a total delivered price quote for the customer, and it would take up too much time with the increased volume of customer requests. Mike was concerned that the new inside salespeople would struggle to compile quotes accurately and correctly and that it would take up way too much of their time, taking them away from other tasks they had to complete.

The solution was to automate the calculations to speed up the process and, at the same time, ensure accuracy. Mike consulted with his accountant, who was an expert in Microsoft Excel. With his accountant's help and advice, Mike created a quoting program that allowed him and his team to compile accurate customer price quotes in seconds instead of taking ten to fifteen minutes. This is a good example of finding a trusted advisor who is an expert with calculations and using a tool such as Microsoft Excel. His advisor's assistance, combined with Mike's hands-on experience with the details, produced a powerful quoting tool that could be updated and continuously improved with input from the team.

Packing orders was a long, expensive process, but the material had to be protected to prevent damage during shipping. Mike was discouraged about the time it took him to pack and protect orders, plus the cost of the effort. Even with the robust packaging, some orders were still damaged in shipping.

There had to be a better way, but he had no idea how to improve it. He shared his frustrations with the drivers from the carrier shipping company he worked with and looked at how other companies handled packaging with the material being shipped inside the same trucks. The drivers offered valuable feedback, and Mike decided to ask the carrier for help. He figured they were packaging experts, and because they were establishing the packaging requirements, they could help with a better solution. He was their customer, and they were his primary shipping vendor, so he thought he would ask for their ideas and expertise at no charge. He recognized that the benefit for the carrier was that orders would be ready on time and the drivers would get loaded faster, saving them both time and money.

The carrier sent over its packaging engineers and developed a better packing solution at a lower cost, allowing orders to be packaged faster and in a way that prevented damage during shipping. Mike did not have anyone on his team to improve this process, so his collaboration with the carrier created an example of creativity over capital and working with a vendor to improve the process at no cost.

When launching the business, Mike arranged to use an extra forklift from another tenant who shared the warehouse. The forklift was old, with limited features and less precision than its newer counterparts. In setting up the warehouse, moving materials, and packing out the first few orders, Mike damaged some materials with the forks. He had to spend extra time to manually adjust the spacing between the forks to accommodate different types of bulk materials and moving orders around in the warehouse.

Mike had past career experience with forklifts and was also concerned about the forklift operating safely for his warehouse team members who would use it daily. Considering Mike's mission to deliver on their customer value proposition, he weighed the pros and cons of acquiring a new forklift. He considered the cost and the needed features and reliability, plus the risk of damage, late orders, and extra time to manually adjust the forks. As the owner and an entrepreneur, he decided that the cost of leasing a new forklift was worth the benefits.

Mike's story illustrates the value of learning by doing and considering the longer-term benefits. His hands-on work gave him the knowledge to make a better business decision in support of their customer value proposition and gave him firsthand knowledge of how long the process of packing and prepping orders for shipment should take.

Another area of Mike and Tim's business that improved during their early growth stage involved their installation instructions. The business sold to do-it-yourself consumers and professional trade customers such as contractors, carpenters, and builders. Mike's experience as a carpenter helped him draft the basic installation instructions for consumers. He recognized that not everyone is confident or has the carpentry skills to install the products themselves. Still, he believed that with detailed guidance in the instructions, many consumers would be able to tackle most types of projects.

The instructions were satisfactory, but he thought they had room for improvement. He often found himself on the phone answering installation questions and helping customers navigate their projects.

He decided to install barnwood accent walls in his office to refine the installation instructions. He also reached out to several customers who were professional carpenter contractors and offered them a discount on their next project order if they would provide feedback and input on improving the installation instructions to make it easier to guide do-it-yourselfers through the installation process. As a result, Mike significantly improved the instructions and spent less time on the phone guiding customers through their projects. This is a creative example of learning by doing, offering a price discount, and enlisting customer experts to improve the do-it-yourself consumer experience.

I may not be great at coming up with new ideas, but I have taken several existing ideas, obsessed over them, and turned them into successful products and services over the years. Some would describe me as an implementer, a maximizer, and a strategic thinker focused (obsessed) on learning and future possibilities.

I have been conditioned as a change agent, which means I thrive on challenging the status quo, asking questions without knowing the answers, and learning by doing. I also enjoy initiating, managing, testing, and implementing changes to processes, systems, or behaviors to drive improvements and motivate others to believe *"We can beat that!"*

Learning, sharing, understanding, and acknowledging each other's strengths helps us work together when we address problems or tackle improvements from different perspectives. As a business owner, this shows your interest in understanding the employees you count on and gives insight into how they approach solving problems and making improvements. Also, sharing your strengths gives them a sense of your approach and fosters productive teamwork toward your stated goals.

Being an owner and entrepreneur does not mean that you must be an expert at everything, but it does mean that you need to understand the details of your business. You cannot improve it until you clearly understand it. Improvement comes in many forms: efficiency, effectiveness, quality, accuracy, customer experience, lower costs, safety, and the employee experience.

Consider the employee experience and encourage open sharing as part of your effort to drive continuous improvement. Providing your employees with the right tools and resources to meet and exceed goals and work standards makes their work easier and less stressful.

Foster an open company culture with a sense of urgency, continuous improvement, and innovation. Challenge yourself and your team to redefine what is possible. When you do, I am confident that *"You can beat that!"*

The next page shows a checklist to help you stay organized with your progress.

HACK 12
SETTLE INTO YOUR NEW HOME

Completed

Have you successfully learned and done every operational job function? ☐

Did you get yourself a whiteboard and a pack of multicolor markers? ☐

Did you and your team take the Gallup StrengthsFinder? ☐

Have you found a trusted advisor and mentor? ☐

Are you prepared to move to the next phase of construction? ☐

HACK 13

MAINTAIN, REPAIR, OR REPLACE
Make Tough Decisions

Eighteen percent of businesses fail within one year, 31 percent of businesses fail after two years, 38 percent of businesses close after three years, and 50 percent of businesses fail after five years.

— SMALL BUSINESS STATISTICS (2024), CHAMBER OF COMMERCE

THE PROBLEM: I AM UNSURE IF I SHOULD CONTINUE WITH A STRUGGLING BUSINESS

WHEN YOU BUILD a new home, significant planning and coordination go into the construction process. From the initial design and blueprints to the move-in day, many details must go well and as planned for a successful home build. So what would happen if you built your new dream home, invested significant time and money in it, moved in, and started to realize that it was laden with many unanticipated issues and problems?

Issues such as subpar workmanship, site problems, and unmet expectations in the quality of the final product could lead to conflicts with the builder and contractors. The overwhelming complexity of these issues—especially if you lack the experience to repair, replace, or address them—combined with the stress of the additional costs and the emotional toll—leads you to question whether it is worth it to cut your losses, sell the house, and move on with your life.

Many startup leaders plan well, launch their new business, and get to the early growth stage before realizing things are not going well. Slow sales growth and underestimated costs can lead to financial and cash flow problems. Operational issues such as inconsistent processes can lead to errors and poor customer service. Hiring the right people can be difficult, causing team conflicts and leading the owner to suffer from burnout from taking on too much and covering for employee shortcomings and mistakes. Established competitors with more resources may take notice and increase their marketing and sales focus, lowering their prices to keep their existing customers. Customer feedback may indicate that the product and service do not adequately meet customer needs. Negative shifts in economic conditions may contribute to slow sales growth and financial issues. All these challenges could have the owners questioning whether they should continue the business or cut their losses and shut it down.

THE HACK: MAINTAIN, REPAIR, OR REPLACE

Almost one in three businesses fail after two years, and half fail within five. Businesses that have been in operation for a long time have had the opportunity to actively learn, pivot, and adjust, learning what does not work, what does work, what they can control, and what they cannot control.

If your business is struggling, we'll want to clarify the answer to one critical question before we jump into problem-solving mode to find the root causes of the troubles. The question is this: **How do you define success?**

After all the research, planning, calculations, operational structure and processes, marketing and sales strategies, funding, and goal-setting you've done so far, the standard answer may sound like this: "My business is successful if we are making money."

Unlike large businesses with many stakeholders and investors, a small business's definition of success can reach beyond short-term financial performance as the sole measure of success. Beyond financial success, think about what you are learning about yourself and your strengths, weaknesses, passion, and motivation. What skills and competencies have you developed to think strategically, adapt, overcome, and make difficult decisions?

What if your business has positive indicators, growing sales, good service and processes, quality products, positive customer feedback, a trusted brand presence, and a team that is confident, motivated, and works well together? Would you define that scenario as success? At the very least, would you consider those qualities as progress?

Financial success is mission-critical, for sure. However, I challenge you to consider the value of your investments, progress, learning milestones, and motivation when deciding whether to continue your business or shut it down and cut your losses.

WHAT YOU CAN DO TOMORROW

Your primary goal is to find the root causes of why your business is struggling and decide whether you *can* and *will* make changes to continue your business or whether it is best to shut it down. Determining the root causes of your business struggles starts with exploring and answering internal company and external market questions.

- **Answer the following internal company questions:**
    - ▸ Do I have a good handle on the finances, and do I effectively manage cash flow?
    - ▸ Do I truly understand my target market?
    - ▸ Are my products or services competitively priced?
    - ▸ What feedback are we getting from customers?
    - ▸ Am I using the most effective marketing strategies to promote my business?

- Have we consistently executed a purposeful sales process aligned with our customer value proposition?
- What is our close rate for turning leads into customers?
- Is my team well-trained, motivated, and working effectively?

- **Answer the following external market questions:**

  - What market changes have occurred since I launched the business?
  - How have economic conditions changed since I launched the business?
  - What has changed with my direct competitors?
  - What new competitive products, services, technologies, or trends have entered the market?
  - What has changed with my target market?
  - Could there be seasonality or timing trends in customer buying decisions?
  - Has the overall market opportunity changed for my product or service?

You may need to ask other questions based on your unique situation and challenges. The prior questions are intended to get you thinking about the internal and external factors, as well as what you can and cannot control.

BUILDING MOMENTUM

The purpose of these thought-provoking questions is to identify the potential problems preventing your business from being successful and then zero in objectively to identify the root cause of those problems, which is preventing the mission-critical deliverable of making money. Here are the key steps of that process.

STEP 1: Make a list of the problems you identified.

You may have identified multiple problems, or only one or two stand out as obvious problems negatively impacting your business. Listing all the problems is important because they are interconnected, and some may result from a more severe problem.

STEP 2: Rank the severity of each problem.

This step aims to identify the most critical problems and their severity, impact, and urgency to address. Use the matrix shown in Table 13.1 to rank the severity of each problem based on its negative effects on the mission-critical deliverable of making money.

Severity of Problem Matrix

Severity	Impact	Urgency
1	Low	Would be nice to fix
2	Modest	Time to address
3	Significant	Needs correction
4	Negative	Have to fix it now
5	Critical	Top priority

Table 13.1

STEP 3: Apply the 5 Whys technique to each identified problem ranked as a 5.

Sakichi Toyoda developed the 5 Whys technique around 1930, and Toyota Motor Corporation used it for quality and efficiency improvements. This problem-solving method involves asking "Why?" five times to uncover the root cause of a problem. It can be applied to any problem.

Applying the 5 Whys technique:

1. Start with the problem statement for each issue labeled as severity 5, critical, and top priority.

2. Ask why. Why is the problem occurring? Write down the answer.

3. Ask why again, based on the answer from the first why.

4. Repeat asking why up to five times or until you identify the root cause.

5. Once you have identified the root cause, you can develop potential solutions and decide if you can solve the problem.

STEP 4: Answer the "Can you and will you?" question.

The first step is to determine whether you can solve a problem. If you can't, making the difficult decision to shut down your business may be easier than struggling on. However, if you determine that you can solve the problem and continue your business, you must consider whether you will execute and implement the potential solution.

REMOVING OBSTACLES

Here are common questions at this stage, with my guidance on how to proceed.

What if I am unsure whether my finances will hold out long enough? Wondering about finances can be a tricky obstacle, and you need to estimate how long it will take to make changes and solve issues to turn the business around, grow sales, and reach a break-even point where you are making enough money to cover expenses. Even if you want to keep your business going, you cannot burn through cash, your business loan, or a line of credit for long.

Nail It:

Determining how long your finances can hold out and how long it will take to make course corrections will require a deep-dive analysis of your finances and profit potential and a reset of your forecast to get to the break-even point. I recommend involving your accountant in the analysis process and leaning on their feedback and guidance.

How can I prepare to make tough decisions? There is no easy way around making tough decisions, and *you* must make them. You will have more decisions to make than whether to continue your business or shut it down. Other examples of difficult decisions include whether to scale back, implement cost-cutting measures such as eliminating or laying off employees (if you have employees), change your product or service, adjust your business model, and modify or overhaul your customer value proposition.

How do I know the potential solution will work? You will not know if your potential solution will work, but you can make informed decisions based on your analysis. Your confidence in how you have learned and developed your competence and expertise in your markets and industry will be a major contributor to your decision to continue your business or shut it down.

What if the root causes are issues that are out of my control? External forces out of your control may be too difficult to overcome. Think of the COVID pandemic and how it impacted many businesses that had to shut down. It's an extreme example, but it illustrates the potential factors out of your control that could lead you to the decision to cut your losses and shut down your business. Another example is when a vendor has a catastrophic event, such as a fire in their plant, and can no longer supply you with a critical component to make your product.

How do I overcome difficult market and economic headwinds? Headwinds in the market and poor economic conditions that negatively impact the market opportunity (customers available to sell to) mean that all companies will take action to secure business from the smaller pool of customers. Larger, established competitors may be in a better financial position to outlast smaller businesses. When all businesses are negatively impacted by market and economic headwinds, nearly every functional area of your business may feel the impact. What is most difficult is trying to predict if the headwinds are short term or long term and if your business can survive with or without significant modifications.

THE HACK IN ACTION

Earlier in my career, I had the privilege of working closely with and supporting roofing contracting businesses. They came in various sizes, from two men and a pickup truck to larger contracting businesses with many installation crews, broader operations, and dedicated sales and marketing teams. Regardless of their size, they competed against each other in their primary business of installing new roofs on homes in the Western Michigan market.

I had known one of the owners of these businesses for several years. He started small but significantly grew his business over the past couple of years. We would typically meet after the holidays to recap the previous year and discuss plans for the upcoming year. Before our next meeting, I was eager to hear how well his business had done now that it was a larger company.

To my surprise, he was stressed, and he expressed concerns that he may have to make significant changes or shut down his business altogether. He said sales were good, but he was working harder than he ever had, and they were not making money. The severity of his problem was definitely level-5 critical. In an informal conversation, I walked through the 5 Whys with him.

1. Why did you not make money last year?
   Answer: Our costs were way too high.

2. Why were costs too high?
   Answer: We needed more people, equipment, trucks, insurance, and so on.

3. Why did you need more people, equipment, trucks, insurance, and so on?

Answer: To support the significant sales growth.

4. Why did you take on such significant sales growth?
   Answer: The growth opportunity was there, and we were just trying to keep up.

5. Why were you just trying to keep up?
   Answer: We scaled up fast and invested in many new resources without being able to cover the expenses through our sales.

Root Cause: The business scaled up too quickly, and he could not effectively manage the growth and maintain sufficient control over the business to make money.

The roofing contractor industry competitors seemed to value and admire the larger businesses, assuming that the larger a company grows, the more successful it would be and the more money it would make.

My friend learned that bigger is not necessarily better. He had a difficult decision to make, and after a thorough evaluation of his six years in business and his financial history, operations, quality of service, expertise, and personal quality of life, he decided to scale back the business and target revenue levels and operations to year three. After scaling back, he made the most money, offered excellent customer service, and had a solid command of his business. He also found a better personal balance in his life.

The following year, with the changes he had made and what he had learned, his business exceeded its income from year three.

FINAL WORD

There is only one thing to do with failure:
learn from it, turn your failure into a beginning
of success. Back up and start over. Often,
the fastest way ahead is to go back.

— PETER KREEFT, AUTHOR AND PROFESSOR OF PHILOSOPHY

STARTING A NEW business is a calculated risk. My hope for *Your Small Business Blueprint* is that it will put your new business in the best possible position to be successful in the early growth stage and to continue to improve. I aim to give you the framework to expand your competence in your business acumen and your expertise in your chosen market and industry.

Every new business owner has to make complex considerations and decisions. I prefer the mindset of learning and preparation, continuous improvement, and quickly adapting to the new business with high energy and high expectations for continued success.

Statistics show that failure is a potential reality for new businesses. Change is constant, and I believe the greatest advantage of a small startup business is its ability to adapt and change *quickly*—not hastily, but by using the structure presented in *Your Small Business Blueprint* to back up, start over, and focus on your competence from what you have learned so you can turn failure into success.

Remember that to keep your startup holding steady financially through the early growth stage, you'll need to have money set aside to cover operating expenses until your sales revenue (and, ideally, profits) can cover your operating expenses each month. In Hack 10, you estimated the number of months of operating expenses you would need to set aside. We touched on factors and conditions that can impact your path to profitability.

Once you are generating monthly profits, what do you do with them?

When the business starts making a profit, acknowledge and celebrate this milestone and then direct the dollars into a safety net fund (operating reserve) to cover monthly operating expenses during periods of uncertainty. I recommend a conservative approach, aiming for a safety net that will cover at least three to six months of operating expenses.

To do this, set up a budget for your monthly profits. This allocation of profits is a strategic and subjective decision for business owners. I recommend a modest approach with the goal of lasting success and allowing for continued investment in the business for growth.

Recommended profit allocation:

- *50 percent for reinvestment*: Set aside this money to reinvest in growth-related expenses (hiring, new products or services, marketing).

- *30 percent for reserves*: Set aside this money in savings until it reaches your targeted months of operating reserve.

- *20 percent for owners and taxes*: Set aside this money for taxes and profit distributions for owners.

Think of your profit allocation as a savings plan to create a stable financial foundation to support the long-term success of your startup through the early growth stage.

CONCLUSION

YOU'RE RUNNING A BUSINESS

A closed mind cannot find new pathways and alternate solutions.

— JEFF BEZOS, FOUNDER OF AMAZON

I HOPE THE THREE lessons in your drive to "figure it out" in structuring and launching your new business have loudly echoed as you worked through *Your Small Business Blueprint*:

1. Learning never stops.

2. Change is constant.

3. Continuous improvement is, well, continuous.

I encourage you to embrace these three lessons and use them early and often to make well-informed decisions that will steer your new business toward lasting success.

As you begin your new business venture, remember that the journey will be filled with opportunities and challenges.

Stay adaptable and open to change while keeping your vision clear and flexible. Focus on deeply understanding your customers, and let their needs shape your decisions.

I'll leave you with these final bits of business wisdom.

Develop your leadership style.

You are the boss and have all the authority to make the decisions and run your business as you want. So, what kind of leader do you want to be? What type of trust do you want to develop with your team? Even if you are a one-person business, you can find value in thinking about what type of business leader you will be. I have asked many leaders I reported to, and I have had many team members ask me, "What is your leadership style?"

I have shared and heard many answers to this question, firmly believing that you lead by example and will not ask anyone on your team to do anything you would not do first. These two answers have shaped my approach to my personal leadership style.

- **It's about little me, big you.** Celebrate wins from the efforts and work of your team, and when it comes to losses, the leader should shoulder the responsibility. Shout praise and whisper criticism. As the leader, you set the tone every day. Start every day with a positive, can-do, *"We can beat that!"* attitude.

- **Lead with curious humility.** This quality directly ties into fostering a culture of learning, continuous improvement, trust, and collaboration with your team. Being humble builds trust and openness. Being curious conveys that you are interested in the details and value their input and contributions. The two most complimentary words to describe a good leader are "curious humility."

Work backward and fail forward.

In all that you do, start with the customer and build your business backward from there. The customer is the primary reason every business exists. If you stay in tune with customer needs, your probability of success goes up significantly. Every business stumbles and makes mistakes with customers. It is what you do when mistakes are made that makes all the difference. Fail forward by going above and beyond to correct your mistakes. Not just because reviews of any business happen early and often but because it is the right thing to do. Over time, this will develop trust in your brand.

Eliminate your own job.

In almost every leadership role in my career, I have shared with my teams that my goal was to eliminate my own job. It sounds strange to profess this, especially if you are on the receiving end as a team member, and I did get some strange looks. I contend that a good leader is not someone to lean on but to make leaning unnecessary. In Hack 3, I shared the quote from Ralph Waldo Emerson: "An institution is the lengthened shadow of one man [person]." This wisdom is true at the launch of your new business and may remain true well into the early growth stage. However, this may not be sustainable for you over time, and it does not allow your team to develop and maximize their value and contributions to the business.

Teach selected and trusted team members to execute your responsibilities successfully. The result will be a stronger company where activities and service to your customers are met and exceeded daily. The advantage for you as the owner is that you can focus more of your time proactively on continuous improvement, innovation, and advancing the business to the next level of growth and profitability.

Go make it happen!

I wish you success in your new venture and hope that *Your Small Business Blueprint* has given you valuable insights and a practical framework to structure and launch your company effectively.

Visit ronneary.com for tools and resources to help advance your startup. I would love to hear how your new business is progressing.

MEET THE AUTHOR

Ron Neary is a high-energy business leader specializing in startups, turnarounds, go-to-market strategies, and profit and process improvement. With a strong track record of driving revenue growth and profitability and enhancing customer service through process improvements, Ron thrives on collaborating with leadership teams to maximize results, deliver world-class customer experiences, and elevate individuals and teams to their highest potential.

Ron leverages his experience and expertise in identifying the root causes of business challenges, developing effective strategies, implementing changes, and creating solutions that help businesses drive revenue, maximize profits, and develop high-performing teams.

He has worked in a diverse range of industries, from architectural products and building materials to electrical solutions and e-commerce. Ron has brought innovative approaches to business challenges and driven significant growth in both product and service organizations.

With a relentless commitment to learning by doing, continuous improvement, and developing pragmatic business solutions, Ron is driven by his core values of curious humility, integrity, responsibility, servant leadership, and strategic thinking. His passion for leadership is reflected in his signature themes from the Gallup CliftonStrengths assessment: Learner, Strategic, Maximizer, Responsibility, and Futuristic—qualities that underscore his dedication to fostering growth and creating meaningful impact for business leaders and their teams.

Website: ronneary.com
Email: ron@ronneary.com
LinkedIn: linkedin.com/in/ron-neary
X: @ronnearycs

ACKNOWLEDGMENTS

To my publishing team

I would like to express my gratitude to the team at Times 10 Publications for allowing me to author and curate *Your Small Business Blueprint*. A special thanks to my project manager, Regina Bell, for her patience and support throughout the process.

To you, a new entrepreneur

I am honored to have the opportunity to serve you, a new entrepreneur seeking support and guidance, as you invest your time, talent, and resources into starting your business.

To Roger Gould

I want to express my gratitude to Roger for being both a mentor and a friend. Having known me for over twenty years, he has played a significant role in my professional and personal growth. We've collaborated on countless projects, and with each one, I gained new and valuable insights.

To the Georgia-Pacific team

In my first professional job after college, Ray, Rick, Frank, and the Teamsters crew placed their trust in me and encouraged me to "figure it out." I am deeply grateful for their positive influence on my early professional growth.

To the Foundation Building Materials team

I want to thank Grant, Rick, and Randy for their confidence, trust, and openness when I was tasked with leading and getting their signature business back on track. The team I was fortunate enough to lead embraced change and delivered.

To David Gushiken

David is a longtime business colleague and friend, and I have never had a teammate who worked as hard or maintained such a "can-do" attitude, even when my ideas, strategies, and initiatives seemed outlandish, maybe even a bit crazy.

To Grandpa Thomas

His mantra, *"Kill them with kindness,"* has resonated with me throughout my life. He taught me the importance of leading by example with kindness, humility, patience, and a commitment to serving others. He understands that I am still a work in progress and that we are all called to strive to be the best version of ourselves every day.

SNEAK PEEK

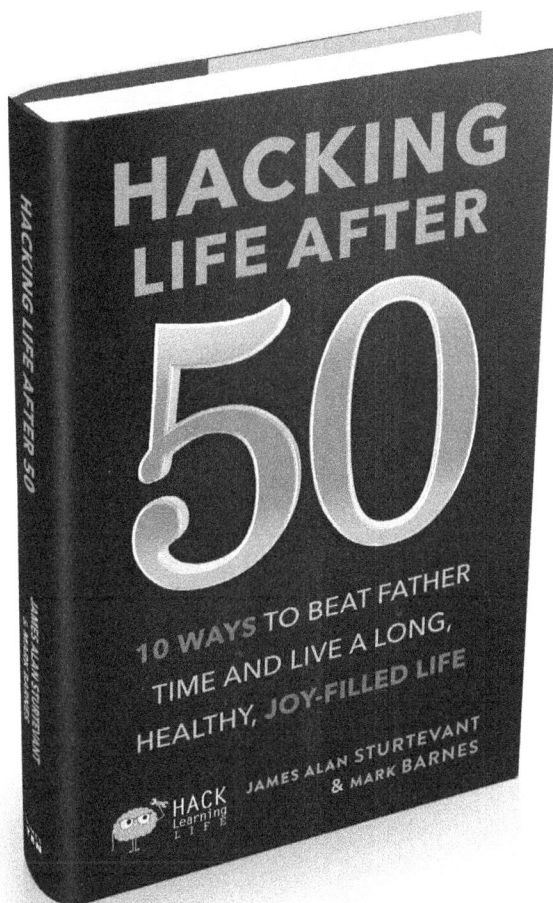

HACKING LIFE AFTER 50

HACKING
LIFE AFTER

50

10 WAYS TO BEAT FATHER
TIME AND LIVE A LONG,
HEALTHY, JOY-FILLED LIFE

HACK
Learning
LIFE

JAMES ALAN STURTEVANT
& MARK BARNES

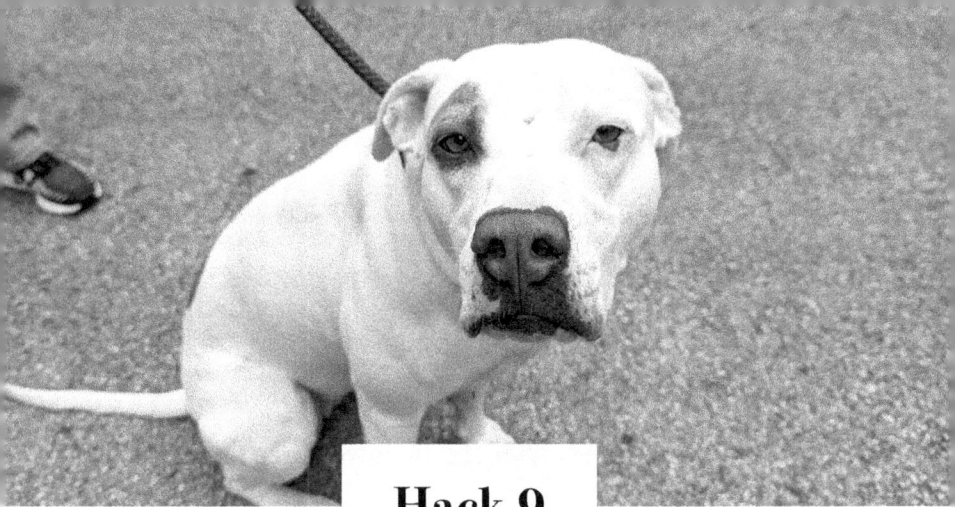

Hack 9

CONNECT
You're not done making friends

The most terrible poverty is loneliness
and the feeling of being unloved.
— MOTHER TERESA, FOUNDER OF
MISSIONARIES OF CHARITY

THE PROBLEM: YOU'RE FEELING ISOLATED

LIFE AFTER FIFTY can be lonely. This is not only sad, but it can also be dangerous. The Centers for Disease Control and Prevention, in an online article titled "Loneliness and Social Isolation Linked to Serious Health Conditions," equated social isolation's health impact to standard villains of longevity such as smoking and obesity. This is a sobering claim. It's time to recognize that isolation, aside from being tragic, is also a threat to health.

Think of all the events that can happen after age fifty that accelerate this isolation:

- Your kids leave home.

- You retire and then miss your coworkers.

- You lose physical mobility, so you aren't as active.

- A relationship dissolves.

- A dear friend moves to be close to their kids.

- Your aged parent dies.

- A beloved sibling dies.

- Your friends start to die.

- Your dog dies.

- Your spouse dies.

- Your familiar neighborhood doesn't seem familiar anymore because your friends are downsizing and moving away.

This list was so easy to make and not meant to be exhaustive. It could go on and on. One of the cruelest aspects to aging is that, as you get older, these isolating factors grow exponentially. When you reminisce about aging and deceased friends and family, you start to wonder, *Will I be the last one standing?* In this life stage, attending and planning memorial services become a painful reality.

One factor that can exacerbate feelings of isolation and loneliness, not to mention envy, is social media. We know many contemporaries who doom-scroll on Facebook almost nightly. They peruse self-promotional posts from acquaintances who seem to have it all. They're off on magnificent vacations, their beautiful families arrange themselves perfectly for group photos at celebrations and holidays, and their carefully selected photos and profile pics make them look twenty years younger.

Please understand that there's probably lots of drama hidden behind these highly scripted and curated billboards of domestic bliss. They likely aren't nearly as content, and their families nearly as congenial, as they look. Your nightly Facebook journeys could, unfortunately, act as painful reminders of everything you don't have and everything you aren't. Such emotions can contribute to feelings of isolation. But we don't want to come off as hypocrites in terms of social media. We've posted self-promotionally. It's fun to share photos you're proud of and have friends celebrate your achievement. Social media also has wonderful aspects and can reunite lost friends and foster new relationships, but we've come to recognize the negative side of these powerful tools. These platforms should serve us, not make us feel bad. We can help you use social media in ways that serve you.

"Social media does have the power to facilitate new relationships and nurture old ones. A great tactic is to utilize direct messaging. My favorite DM strategies are to send a congratulation when a friend shares an accomplishment (even if I'm a little envious) and a condolence when a friend faces a hardship or loss. My experience has been that such messages make the recipients feel good and lead to more interactions between them and me. That's a great use of social media."

Coming to grips with the bitter realities of this life stage and dealing with feelings of envy that everyone else is thriving because of what they post on social media is hard enough. What's doubly challenging is to figure out how to break out of your After-50s isolation and rejoin the world. If you're retired, you've lost the social interaction opportunity that came by default at work each day. If you're not retired, you know what to expect in your not-too-distant future. Are you cognizant that the extensive social network you interact with daily will dwindle to a trickle? What preparations are you making for this loss? The previous sentence articulates what we'll attempt to do in this Hack.

Meeting and socializing with people probably happened organically for most of your life. You met people at work. You met people at church. You met people through your kid's activities. You became friends with your neighbors who were at a similar life stage. Now that you're after fifty, it's important for you to be intentional about connecting. The same skill sets you utilized when you were younger to find the right job or the right spouse can now be resurrected and then adapted to the goal of finding new friends. The great news is that, compared to interviewing for a job or proposing to a potential spouse, finding new friends after fifty is a low-stakes aspiration. If you attempt to connect with a new friend and the interaction fizzles, you're out virtually nothing and you can learn a lot about how to improve your search filter. And, you're not attempting to find just one dream job or just one soulmate. There's a lot less pressure when you're just trying to interact with more people and find new friends.

THE HACK: CONNECT

It's helpful to think about connection as capital. When economists talk about capital, they're referring to assets. Acquiring new friends *is* acquiring new assets. New friends are valuable. They can make you happier and healthier. They can be there for you in a crisis. You can be as beneficial to them as they are to you. We have plenty of friends who are contemporaries and consider us as assets. So we're going to stick with our analogy.

As we mentioned in The Problem section of this Hack, our desire is to spark intentionality about connecting. That's not to say that new friendships cannot blossom organically; we just don't want you to sit idly by, waiting for someone else to make the first move. That probably didn't work decades ago at your high school dances unless, of course, you were smoking hot, and it probably won't work at this stage of life. We aim to give you some ideas, but we're more concerned with helping you find the motivation and the confidence to step out of your comfort zone and make the first move. We won't just yell, *Get over your fears and get out there!* Instead, we want to inspire you to get out there in your own time and in your own way.

To bond with others, you need to be approachable. Have you ever evaluated your approachability? Do you broadcast a welcoming vibe? Would you feel comfortable meeting you? These are important questions, and adjustments in this realm could be instrumental in achieving a broader social network.

As with all the Hacks in this book, we encourage you to create your own goals and your own roadmap to expand your connections—and we'll offer many suggestions along the way. This is ultimately your journey, but sometimes you need a nudge in the right direction. This Hack works hand-in-hand with Hack 8. Often, the pursuit of engagement leads to opportunities to expand your social interactions with like-minded people. As with engagement, networking is an invaluable tool.

And finally, even though the focus of this Hack is to grow your social network, you probably have more relationships than you think. Those bonds with friends and family need to be nurtured and maintained. Please don't take these important folks for granted.

SNEAK PEEK

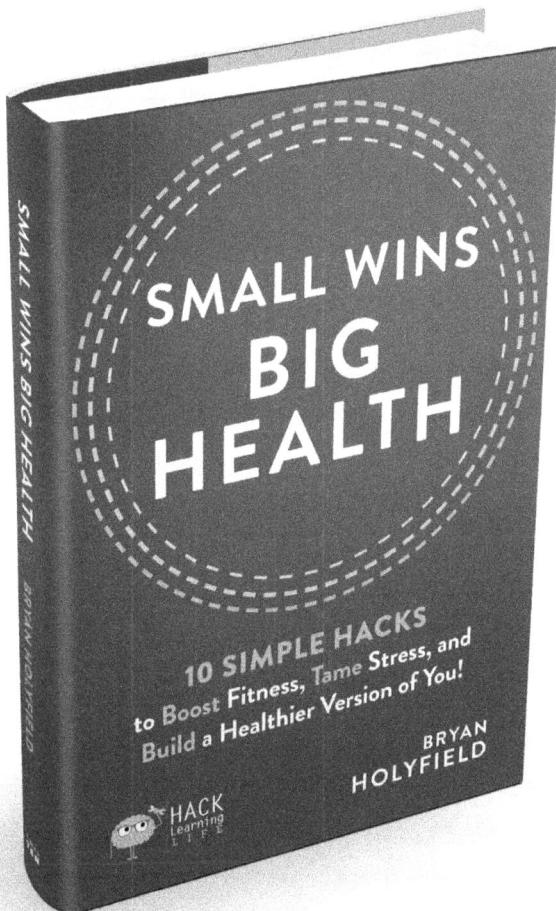

(HACK 3)

EAT LIKE YOU MEAN IT

Eat On Purpose for Balance and Sustainability

The table is a meeting place, a gathering ground,
the source of sustenance and nourishment,
festivity, safety, and satisfaction.
— LAURIE COLWIN, AUTHOR

THE PROBLEM: WE EAT FOR CONVENIENCE AND COMFORT

I N TODAY'S FAST-PACED society, convenience often takes precedence over proper nutrition, leading to detrimental effects on general health and increasing stress and anxiety surrounding food, what we should and shouldn't eat, and dicting habits.

At the core of the issue is the prevalence of fast food, highly processed meals, and snacks that have become staples in our diets. These foods are often highly palatable and high in unhealthy fats and added sugars while lacking essential nutrients like fiber, vitamins, and minerals.

The convenience-focused culture surrounding food choices also promotes mindless eating and a disconnect from the actual process of nourishing your body. Eating on the go, in front of screens, or in a rushed manner diminishes the enjoyment and mindfulness associated with meals. The convenience of grabbing a quick meal on the go or ordering takeout has led to a significant decline in home-cooked, wholesome meals. Food is an object of fixation and often devoid of the pleasure of being prepared in the home and part of engaging in communal dining experiences.

This overreliance on quick fixes has resulted in a range of negative health impacts. The consumption of highly processed foods contributes to the rising rates of obesity, heart disease, diabetes, and other chronic conditions. These health problems not only affect individuals but also place a significant burden on the healthcare system.

Furthermore, the lack of balance in the American diet has a direct correlation with stress levels. The constant intake of high-sugar, high-fat foods can lead to energy crashes, mood swings, and decreased mental clarity. Along with high stress, overconsumption, and health concerns comes the ever-increasing presence of weight loss marketing and misinformation about healthy approaches to nutrition. Weight loss marketing and the diet culture at large often fall short in addressing the lack of proper nutritional education, how to navigate necessary lifestyle changes, the importance of macronutrients and micronutrients, and individualized metabolic needs. In a society focused on convenience, quick fixes, and the pursuit of an idealized body, diet culture promotes restrictive eating patterns and unrealistic expectations, leading to frustrations and feelings of hopelessness for many who strive to achieve optimal health.

One major issue with diet culture is its tendency to promote fad diets and restrictive eating patterns that often lack scientific evidence and fail to provide adequate nutrition. These diets tend to focus on short-term weight loss goals rather than long-term sustainable health. They often eliminate entire food groups or severely restrict calorie intake, leading to potential nutrient deficiencies, imbalances, or eating disorders.

Moreover, diet culture often overlooks the importance of understanding macronutrients and their role in supporting overall health. While the focus may be on counting calories or eliminating certain foods, the emphasis on macronutrient composition and balance is often neglected. Each macronutrient (carbohydrates, proteins, and fats) plays a crucial role in energy production, hormone regulation, and cellular function. Without some understanding of these macronutrients and their impact on the body, individuals may inadvertently compromise their metabolic needs.

THE HACK: EAT LIKE YOU MEAN IT

Combating the widespread normalization of overconsumption, convenience-focused food culture, and restrictive dieting is a macro-sized problem that can only be addressed at the micro level. It will start with you—with your habits and within your home. Only when you decide enough is enough, take control of what is within your control, and make learning a bit more about nutrition a priority will you find a balanced and sustainable approach to eating mindfully that works for you and your goals.

There is no one-size-fits-all approach to nutrition. There are key principles of nutrition that every individual will benefit from understanding, and there are simple strategies that help make those principles practical to deploy. The ultimate priority is for you to know how to ditch harmful eating habits and gradually replace them with solutions that feel aligned and doable for life. Uncontrolled eating, mindless eating, convenience-focused eating, and overly restrictive eating won't allow you to feel aligned or healthy in the long term. With that common understanding, it's time to dive into core principles of nutrition that are fundamental to a healthy approach to eating.

Food is your source of energy. Some energy sources fuel different aspects of your bodily functions, just like different fluids and oils help a car engine operate effectively. Macronutrients (protein, carbs, and fats) are the three primary categories of energy. Macros are forms of chemical energy, and calories are simply a measure of that energy. A well-balanced diet will include a substantial amount of all three categories of energy. One example of a balanced approach that is manageable for most people is 25 percent protein, 50 percent carbs, and 25 percent fats.

- Proteins are made up of complex chains of essential amino acids. Protein is vital in building all body tissues, including muscle synthesis and hormone and enzyme production. One gram of protein contains a total of 4 calories.

- Carbohydrates also contain 4 calories per gram and are broken down into glucose. Glucose is transported to cells and converted into ATP (adenosine triphosphate) through anaerobic glycolysis.

- Fats contain 9 calories per gram. Fat repels water and is the carrier for the fat-soluble vitamins A, D, E, and K. Fat is another key source of energy through ATP. Our brains are 60 percent fat, and adequate fat intake is necessary for balanced hormone production. We are always burning and always storing fat as adipose tissue to use as energy when required.

Understanding the basics of macronutrients and how the body uses them further illustrates the importance of nutrient-dense foods. If food is fuel, then nutrient-dense foods are better sources of fuel than foods that have been stripped of their nutritional value. Eating mostly nutritionally deficient foods will rob your body of key micronutrients, increase mental and metabolic stress, impede normal digestive functions and gut health, lower your body's immune system and ability to fight inflammation, and increase the potential of many other associated health risks.

Highly processed foods lack the structural and nutritional complexity of whole foods. These foods include what we generally call junk foods but can also include plenty of options that the general public would consider to be "healthier" foods. There are six key markers, or red flags, I teach my clients to look out for in their diets. These markers typically show up in combinations. The higher the number of red flags a food or type of food contains, the more cautious you should be about eating it. The markers are 1) high saturated fat content, 2) high sugar content, 3) high-calorie foods with little nutritional value (check the label for macronutrient and micronutrient info), 4) easier to overeat (not satiating), 5) highly processed, and 6) high flavor stimuli.

Let's dive into simple strategies for swapping foods with these markers for better quality foods that are less processed and more nutritionally rich. A great place to start is to complete a basic food log for three to five days. Simply record everything you consume over this time period without judgment or changing from your existing routine. After completing the food log, you will perform a self-audit. Which foods with multiple red flags show up for you most often? Put these foods into your "red" column. We will dive into this in more detail in the Building Momentum section, but your red-column foods are the ones you need to put more boundaries around to protect your long-term health. This doesn't mean you can never have these foods. It does mean you should focus some energy on finding healthier alternatives as go-to options and save your red-column foods for specific occasions. Visit

If food is fuel, then nutrient-dense foods are better sources of fuel than foods that have been stripped of their nutritional value.

holyfitcoaching.com/smallwins to download free resources, including an ultimate snack guide.

The second major swap is to replace a select number of meals purchased outside the home with ones prepared by you at home. If you consume three or more meals per week from restaurants, fast food, food trucks, or food delivery, you are giving up control of a significant percentage of your meals in terms of portion sizes, quality of ingredients, caloric intake, and impulse control. Even swapping one meal per week is an effective place to start. You can build to a point where dining out is a special occasion or event and not an active part of your lifestyle. Also, begin to emphasize the importance of home-cooked meals over processed and pre-packaged foods. Cooking at home allows you to have control over the ingredients, portion sizes, and cooking methods, ensuring healthier choices and practicing balanced nutrition.

To move away from convenience-focused meals to home-cooked meals, you will need a process for mindful meal planning. Start by creating a weekly meal plan that includes a few staple "go-to" ingredients that can be combined to create a variety of nutritious and balanced meals. Consider the nutritional value, portion sizes, and ingredients when designing your menu. Pick two to three great protein sources, two to three high-quality carb sources, two to three vegetables you enjoy, and two to three healthy fats. For example, a basic shopping list might look like this:

Protein: eggs, chicken breast, lean ground turkey

Carbs: sweet potatoes, brown rice, chickpeas

Vegetables: spinach, carrots, red cabbage

Fats: avocado, extra virgin olive oil, chopped almonds

With these few ingredients, you can mix and match, creating delicious meals to eat at home and to pack for when you are out and about. I love the 3-3-3 model, shown in Image 1, for keeping meals balanced and varied.

3-3-3 STRATEGY

Keep things simple your first few weeks of meal prep. Try the 3-3-3 Method. Choose 3 different protein sources, 3 fat sources, and 3 carb sources only

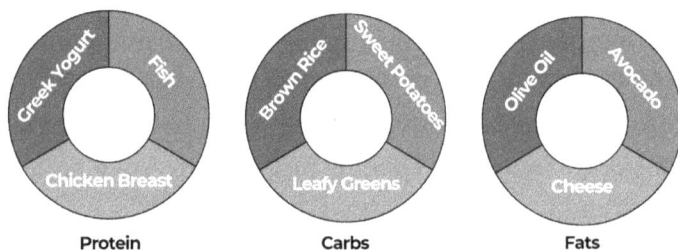

Protein — Carbs — Fats

Image 1

Simply identifying your problem foods, swapping restaurant meals for meals at home, and creating a simple meal plan you can actually follow will take you far in becoming more mindful of your eating habits. But you don't have to do this alone. Seek support and inspiration from other people who are committed to the same process, hire a nutrition coach, and join communities or online groups that promote healthy eating habits. Share recipes, meal ideas, and success stories to stay motivated and inspired. Renowned leadership expert John C. Maxwell said, "The better you are at surrounding yourself with people of high potential, the greater your chance for success." Find your community of people who will spur you on, challenge you, and keep you going on those tough days. (For more meal-planning strategies and ideas, check out the "Master Meal Planning" chapter in the book *Hacking Life After 50* by James Alan Sturtevant and Mark Barnes.)

BUY

HACKING LIFE AFTER 50

AND

SMALL WINS, BIG HEALTH

.

GET *LIFE HACKS* IN YOUR INBOX EVERY SUNDAY MORNING.

Life Hacks include practical, entertaining content that helps you live a better life. They are filled with simple solutions you can read today and use tomorrow ... and they are free. Sign up now at hacklearninglife.com.

TIMES 10 PUBLICATIONS provides practical solutions that busy people can read today and use tomorrow. We bring you content from experienced researchers and practitioners, and we share it through books, podcasts, webinars, articles, events, and ongoing conversations on social media. Our books and materials help turn practice into action. Stay in touch with us at HackLearningLife.com and 10Publications.com and follow our updates @10Publications.